How to Use

MICROSOFT
INTERNET
EXPLORER

How to Use

MICROSOFT INTERNET EXPLORER

SHERRY GORDON HUBERT AND RICH SCHWERIN

Ziff-Davis Press
An imprint of Macmillan Computer Publishing USA
Emeryville, California

Acquisitions Editor	Suzanne Anthony
Development Editor	Kim Haglund
Copy Editor	Deborah Craig
Technical Reviewer	Mark Hall
Production Editor	Barbara Dahl
Book Design	Dennis Gallagher/Visual Strategies, San Francisco
Page Layout	M.D. Barrera and Janet Piercy
Indexer	Valerie Robbins

Ziff-Davis Press, ZD Press, and the Ziff-Davis Press logo are trademarks or registered trademarks of, and are licensed to Macmillan Computer Publishing USA by Ziff-Davis Publishing Company, New York, New York.

Ziff-Davis Press imprint books are produced on a Macintosh computer system with the following applications: FrameMaker®, Microsoft® Word, QuarkXPress®, Adobe Illustrator®, Adobe Photoshop®, Adobe Streamline™, MacLink® *Plus*, Aldus® FreeHand™, Collage Plus™.

Ziff-Davis Press, an imprint of
Macmillan Computer Publishing USA
5903 Christie Avenue
Emeryville, CA 94608

ISBN 1-56276-436-5

Manufactured in the United States of America
10 9 8 7 6 5 4

TABLE OF CONTENTS

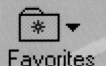

ACKNOWLEDGMENTS

 If this book wasn't written in blood it's only because it was written in sweat and tears. The grueling race against time will not be soon forgotten by the relentless Ziff-Davis Press team who had to endure three beta cycles, painful deadlines, and authors who kept disappearing on business trips just as chapters were due.

We're eternally grateful to Suzanne Anthony, whose patience had run out around Chapter 3, but still managed to hide her frustrations from us and encouraged us to no ends; Lucresia Ashford was infinitely helpful and cooperative; Deborah Craig kept us going with her keen eye, brilliant observations, and an occasional praise; Mark Hall did his best not to shred our manuscripts to pieces though we all knew how badly he wanted to; Kelly Green was constantly cheerful (but then again, ten weeks on a road trip and away from this project might have had something to do with that); Kim Haglund kept her cool amidst an incredible maelstrom; and Barbara Dahl was as accommodating and helpful as we could have wished for.

We're also very grateful to Matt Lake, who came through as a champion, delivering a terrific chapter (we expected no less), and on deadline, too. In fact, it was the only chapter that got filed on time.

But all told, it's been fun. We got to browse some great Web sites and chatted with some pretty weird folks. And now it's your turn.

S. G. Hubert and Rich Schwerin
August 13, 1996

CHAPTER 1

Getting to Know the Internet and the World Wide Web

"Knowledge is the most democratic source of power."
—*Alvin Toffler*

The Internet is, by far, one of the most amazing tools available to humans since the beginning of time. No, this is not an exaggeration. With some relatively inexpensive equipment (a computer, a modem, and a telephone line) you can find information about practically anything, at any time, because the Internet is fast becoming a repository of the sum total of human knowledge.

No less incredible is the fact that, for people online, the world doesn't have borders. You can meet people from the most exotic corners of the earth, even develop meaningful relationships with people you'll never meet face to face. And with such global friendships comes the promise of peace and prosperity.

But enough of that pompous stuff. The truth is, the Internet is where you can find out all the latest gossip about Sandra Bullock or Kevin Costner. It's where you go shopping for hats or book airline flights. It's where you stay up all night chatting with strangers when you can't fall asleep. It's cool, fun, exciting, and, best of all, it's affordable.

What Is the Internet?

S o what's the Internet? It's a galaxy of thousands and thousands of computers, all over the world, all speaking the same language (also known as Internet Protocol), all connected to each other via a common *infrastructure* that is mostly maintained by phone and cable companies. Surprisingly enough, there's nobody in charge. There's no Internet Corporation, no Office of the Internet, no law, no sheriff. It's the Wild West all over again, only this time, the whole world's hitching that covered wagon (so watch out for the traffic jams on the information superhighway!). Oddly enough, this anarchy makes sense.

1 Despite the fact that nobody "owns" or "runs" the Internet (the "Net" for short), the cabling and other connection methods are maintained by telephone companies such as AT&T and MCI. That's the foundation that holds everything together, or, in Net lingo, it's the *backbone*.

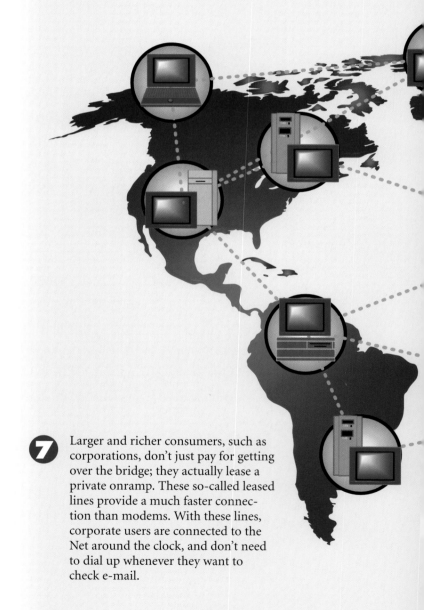

7 Larger and richer consumers, such as corporations, don't just pay for getting over the bridge; they actually lease a private onramp. These so-called leased lines provide a much faster connection than modems. With these lines, corporate users are connected to the Net around the clock, and don't need to dial up whenever they want to check e-mail.

TIP SHEET

▶ **Since the 1996 Telecommunications bill, phone companies themselves have become ISPs.**

▶ **Expect your local cable company to become an Internet provider soon.**

▶ **See the appendix for information about finding Internet service providers (ISPs) in you area.**

2 In reality, there's more than one backbone, as each of these companies maintains its part separately. That's the beauty of the Net: If one part crashes, the others will continue to chug along independently.

3 In fact, the Net is designed to withstand all kinds of nasty blows. The Net was conceived back in the sixties as a way to connect the government, research labs, and universities so that these crucial organizations could continue to function and interact in case of a nuclear attack.

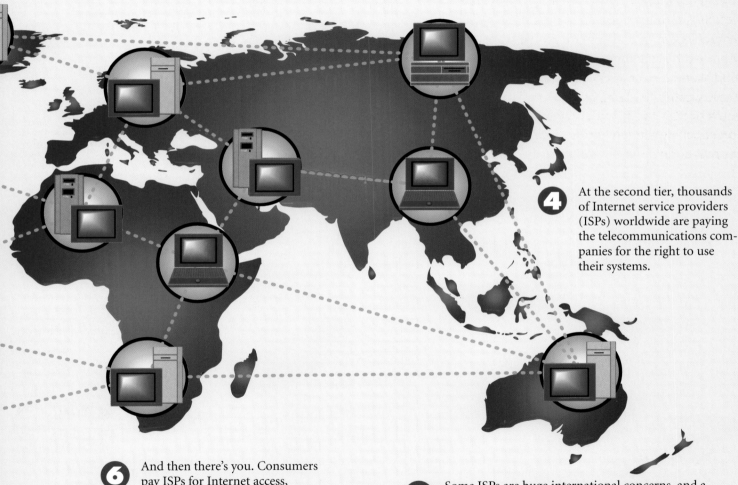

4 At the second tier, thousands of Internet service providers (ISPs) worldwide are paying the telecommunications companies for the right to use their systems.

6 And then there's you. Consumers pay ISPs for Internet access, whether according to usage or a flat monthly fee. Mind you, ISPs aren't just the bridge toll collectors. They provide a value-added service in the way of necessary software, technical support, and other much-needed services.

5 Some ISPs are huge international concerns, and a few are owned by teenagers and operated out of their bedrooms. The majority, however, are medium-sized providers who have a few hundred or a few thousand subscribers. The example closest to your PC is probably the Microsoft Network (MSN), which is using the UUnet backbone. UUnet is a "Super Provider" of sorts, offering Internet access to other ISPs, instead of directly to customers.

What's on the Internet?

The Internet is the ultimate public library. You pay to get in, but in most cases, you can browse books and even take them home without paying extra. I know, I know. This sounds pretty dull. But it's not. In reality, the Net is a lot like a gigantic Barnes and Noble store: lots of great books; a Starbucks coffee shop where you can sip, read, and socialize; poetry readings; book signing; children's story time; and a music area. Now throw in several theme parks, hotel rooms with television sets and telephones, and you've got yourself the Internet. This page describes how these things appear on the Net.

World Wide Web

▶ **1** The World Wide Web (WWW) is by far the most popular part of the Net. It's graphical and intuitive, allowing users to interact with data, not just read it. "Pages," or documents, on the Web may contain text, graphics, animation, video clips, sound, and links to other pages, called *hypertext* links (or just plain hyperlinks). The language of the Web is called HTTP, or Hypertext Transfer Protocol. To view and interact with Web pages you need a Web browser, such as Internet Explorer. See the next page for more information about the Web.

Telnet

6 Telnet is another dying Net breed. It used to be that you could only get on the Net via this cryptic method. You logged on, or *telnetted*, to your server, and then needed to know a bit of the—ugh—UNIX language to get around. Nowadays, only supergeeks use Telnet. Yes, including yours truly. There's just no need for it anymore. The Web with its pretty face has made Telnet obsolete.

TIP SHEET

▶ **The Net is constantly evolving. Although user-friendly tools such as Web browsers have made it easy on mere mortals to go online, there are still remnants of the old ways (such as Gopher) here and there. The important thing to remember is that they don't change the way you work, because your Web browser is here to shield you from the unknown.**

**File
Transfer
Protocol**

2 Before there was the Web, there was FTP, or File Transfer Protocol. FTP allows users to download files from other computers to their own system, and vice versa. FTP is still a major part of the Net, although you don't need to rely on cryptic software to download files, because your Web browser supports FTP. When you used FTP in the old days, you didn't see the files you were downloading; you only saw lists of files. When using your Web browser to download files from FTP sites, in contrast, you can view files and then download them just by clicking if you like what you see.

Gopher

3 Gopher used to be the only way to find files on the Net. Whenever you needed to find some information, you sent a query to a Gopher server, which told you where you needed to go to find what you were looking for. Web search engines are fast making Gopher obsolete (see Chapter 7 for more information), but every once in a while you'll still run into a Gopher site. How can you tell? The URL will start with gopher:// instead of http://.

E-mail

4 E-mail is one of the most popular services on the Net. If you think that the art of letter writing is dead, guess again. Because e-mail reaches its recipients within hours or even minutes, people are writing to each other at a dizzying pace, often several times a day. This instant gratification means that even hopeless procrastinators such as yours truly reply to their mail without delay.

Usenet · E-mail · File Transfer Protocol · Gopher · Telnet · World Wide Web

**Usenet
Newsgroups**

5 Usenet is a system of newsgroups, or discussion groups with bulletin boards and e-mail. It's a great place to meet people and exchange views. To use it, you need a newsreader, or special software for reading and writing newsgroup messages. See Chapter 10 for more information.

How Does the Web Work?

The World Wide Web is the youngest part of the Internet, and the one most responsible for the Internet's popularity. Before the Web came to be, the Internet was largely inaccessible to mere mortals, because navigating it required computer expertise and a great deal of determination. The Web introduced an easy-to-use system, which relies on plain English and lots of graphics to make itself hospitable to the users. Web "pages" are created with HTML, which stands for Hypertext Markup Language. HTML makes it very simple to go from one page to another by clicking on hyperlinks. Here's how.

 1 The Disney Web site includes several hyperlink elements you can click on. Each hyperlink takes you to a different Web page, either on the same site or on a completely different site, perhaps even in a different country. Just click, and you're in Tahiti. One more click, and you're in your home town. You can tell that your mouse is pointing at a hyperlink because the pointer changes from an arrow to a pointing hand.

 6 OK, one more click and we're done. Where are we? How did we get here? Who knows. It's been a while since we started this voyage…. (If you're getting dizzy from jumping so far so fast, don't worry. Chapter 4 explains more about how to travel smoothly to and fro in cyberspace.)

TIP SHEET

▶ You never know where you'll end up when you click on a link. Some Web pages provide little original content, but contain lots of links to other sites, while others offer links to pages on their own site.

▶ Web pages may link you to ftp sites, e-mail addresses, or newsgroups, not just to other Web pages.

▶ Do you enjoy random browsing? Then you'll love the Web. But if you're looking for particular site or bit of information, focus your search using a *search engine*, as described in Chapter 7.

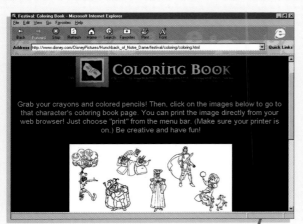

2 Clicking on the Hunchback's image takes you to this page.

3 Clicking on Winners Circle puts you on this page. That underlined text in a different color is the most common way to display hypertext links.

4 Clicking on the family.com hyperlink seems to take us to a completely different site. Total time getting there: 1 second.

5 Click on Travel, and…. By now you got the idea, right? The knee bone's connected to the thigh bone, the thigh bone's connected to the hip bone, and so on. Welcome to the world of the hip-and-with-it!

Things You Can Do on the Web (and on the Net)

So now you know that the Web is a whole lot of "pages" linked together. But what's the point? Is it just a series of useless documents with pretty pictures?

Far from it. There's so much great stuff on the Web, that the useful outweighs the fluff. Whether you're an adult or child, college graduate or high school student, doctor or mechanic, the Web has a lot to enhance your professional, as well as personal, life. Here are a few examples.

TIP SHEET

▶ Curious how to get to these sites? Here are their URLs. When you've gone through Chapter 4, try these out for yourself:

The Dorothy Parker quote can be found at http://www.webbuild.com/~mbowen/sonowuff.htm

The Four11 directory is at http://www.four11.com

For flight information check out http://www.sys1.com

To find out which movies are playing in your area, go to http://www.movielink.com

Sports news (and stats, and other data) are everywhere on the Net. Try Sports Illustrated, for starters, at http://pathfinder.com/si/

You can order flowers from FTD's site (among others) at http://www.ftd.com/

And the Library of Congress is at http://www.loc.gov

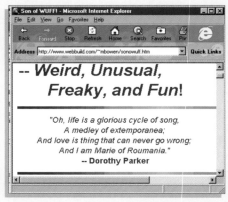

1 Need to settle a bet or get a quick answer for a report you're putting together? Trying to remember who said the immortal words, "…love is a thing that can never go wrong; and I am Marie of Roumania"? Forget your dusty encyclopedia. The Web has it.

8 Are you a news addict? Read the news online, as often as you want, because online "newspapers" update the information on their sites much more often than they do their print version.

7 Are you lonely tonight? No need to be. There are hundreds of thousands of people who are just dying to talk to you. Go online and chat about your favorite topic. Make friends (or enemies), and find out why they say that the Web is the '90s version of a singles bar.

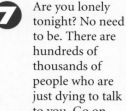

2 Whatever happened to your first flame? Is he/she married? Where does she/he live nowadays? If this person is as smart as you remember, he/she must have an e-mail address; so play detective on the Web.

3 Don't like your travel agent? Dump him. You can plan trips, even book flights and hotel rooms on the Web.

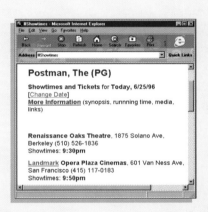

4 What's playing in your neighborhood movie theater? Go online to find out listings, including show times.

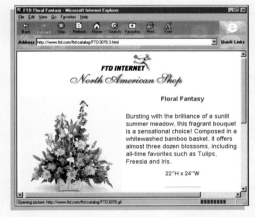

6 Oh, no! You didn't forget your anniversary again, did you? Don't worry. Find the bouquet you like, fill in an electronic card, and give the cyberflorist your credit card number. Your spouse will get the flowers at work, and all will be forgiven. In fact, you can buy practically anything online.

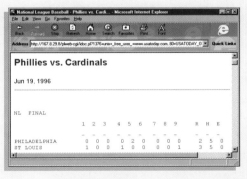

5 So how did the Mets do this afternoon? Find sports results on the Web, along with all the important stats, as soon as they happen.

CHAPTER 2

Installing Internet Explorer

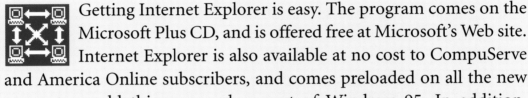 Getting Internet Explorer is easy. The program comes on the Microsoft Plus CD, and is offered free at Microsoft's Web site. Internet Explorer is also available at no cost to CompuServe and America Online subscribers, and comes preloaded on all the new computers sold this year and as part of Windows 95. In addition, Microsoft recently announced the availability of a $19.99 "Internet Starter Kit" CD that includes Internet Explorer, several other programs mentioned in this book (NetMeeting, Internet Mail, Internet News, and more), and 30 free hours on MSN, Microsoft's own Internet access service. If you don't currently have Web access or an account with CompuServe or AOL, this kit is a great way to get started.

Unfortunately, because of this wide variety of options, there's more than one way to install Internet Explorer onto your system. This chapter shows you just one method (installing files downloaded from Microsoft's Web site), but other than the first step, the information is the same regardless of where you get your copy of Internet Explorer.

How to Install Internet Explorer

If Internet Explorer came preloaded on your new system, you're off the hook. But if it came with another program (such as the disk you got from your Internet service provider), here's what you need to do to install it.

msie30.exe

 Find the file MSIE30.EXE on the disk or CD. Double-click on it to start the installation.

TIP SHEET

- ▶ If, after you've rebooted, you get an Internet Connection Wizard dialog box, skip to the next topic for further information.

- ▶ If you already have access to the Internet, you can download Internet Explorer from Microsoft's site, http://www.microsoft.com/ie.

- ▶ If you use CompuServe or America Online, follow those services' instructions for downloading and configuring Internet Explorer.

- ▶ You can download Internet Explorer by itself or combined with Internet Mail and News, and NetMeeting (see Chapters 9, 10, and 15 for more information). My advice: If you're using a modem connection, get these programs one by one, because you'll spend many hours waiting for the combined files to download.

2 The Setup program asks you to confirm that you want to proceed with the installation. Click on Yes to continue.

The Setup program starts by "extracting" several files that have been combined and compressed into MSIE30.EXE.

3

4 Since Internet Explorer is free, Microsoft wants you to read the software license that says, in plain English: "Keep your hands off this program. Don't sell it, don't take it apart, just use it for its intended purpose—browsing the Internet." Unless you click on I Agree, you won't be able to use the program. Click on it now.

6 When the installation is over, you're asked to restart your computer. Before you do, move your pointer to the taskbar, check which applications you currently have open, and close them one by one, saving unsaved documents if necessary. Then click on Yes and your system will reboot.

Relax while files are installed into your system.

5

How to Use the Internet Connection Wizard

Now that Internet Explorer is installed, you need to tell your system how you want to get on the Net—that is, who's your Internet service provider (ISP), what's your ID, what's your password, and so on. If you haven't accessed the Internet with this system, the Internet Connection Wizard dialog box appears automatically. If you have accessed the Net before, Windows 95 assumes that you're keeping the same ISP and doesn't display this dialog box. If you want to supply new information, you can call up the Internet Connection Wizard as described here.

▶ ❶ If, following a successful installation, you got the screen shown at the center of the page, skip to the next step. Otherwise, click on the Start button, select Programs, Accessories, Internet Tools, and Get on the Internet. You'll see the Wizard shown at the center of the page.

❾ You're done! To log on to the Internet, double-click on the Internet Explorer icon on your desktop, which will launch the Internet Dialer you've just configured.

❽ The next three screens will ask you for some highly cryptic information, such as IP Address (your own "address" on the Internet) and other details—all provided by your ISP. If at any point you're asked for information you don't have, call your ISP's customer support hotline.

TIP SHEET

▶ **If you have an account with AOL, CompuServe, or the Microsoft Network, your setup may look a bit different from what you see here.**

▶ **If any of your information ever changes, just repeat the process outlined here.**

2 Click on Next, click on Manual, click on Next, and then click on Next again in the next dialog box.

3 Next you'll need to tell the Wizard whether you're using a modem connection or your company's local area network. If you're using a modem connection, click on Next. If you're using your company's LAN, consult your company's technical support (or MIS) staff for help.

4 Click on Next when asked whether you want to use Windows messaging (to enable e-mail).

5 Type the name of your Internet service provider (in my case, it's DNAI) and click on Next.

7 Type your user ID and password, provided to you by your ISP. The password won't show on the screen as you type it, to protect you from snoops.

6 Next type your ISP's dial-up number and click on Next.

CHAPTER 3

Getting to Know Internet Explorer

 At this point in the book, you're probably dying to fly solo to the mysterious land called the Web. But be patient. You're still just a rookie, and before you can take off, you must become familiar with your equipment.

Fortunately, Internet Explorer isn't as complicated as a jet airplane, or even a single-engine aircraft. You've got your "control panel" with a few buttons, menus, keyboard shortcuts, and that's about it. Once you get the hang of these, you'll be off and cruising in no time (in fact, in Chapter 4). So buckle up, turn on the music, and let's look around the cockpit.

Find Your Way around Internet Explorer

Before you use a tool, you should know what it's called. I mean, Tim "The Tool Man" Taylor would never say to Al, "Hand me that red thingie," would he? So look at the screen at the center of the page and become familiar with the different parts that make it a Web browser.

▶ **❶** The icons on the toolbar are grayed out when they are not in use. When you move your pointer over any icon, it gets a nice sculpted looking button underneath, and color in its cheeks. Once a button looks that way, just click on it once to activate it. In Windows, a button gets one click, while an icon gets a double-click. Why? Just because. The difference between icons and buttons is very little: icons don't have the "sculpted," 3-D look that buttons have.

TIP SHEET

▶ If you've used any Microsoft product before (Windows 95, Word, and so on), you'll be very familiar with the Internet Explorer environment, because Microsoft's products all sport a similar look.

▶ Check out the next four pages for more specific information about the different parts of Internet Explorer's *user interface*.

2 Microsoft doesn't just want you to use its software, it also wants you to rely on it for *content.* So you get these links to generally interesting and useful sites, in addition to some "subtle" hints that you should check out Microsoft's products.

3 The Address box is where you'll type the address (or "URL") of a page you want to visit. Confused by URLs? Check the section "How to Use the Address Bar" at the end of this chapter for more details.

Address box   **Menu bar**   **Toolbar**

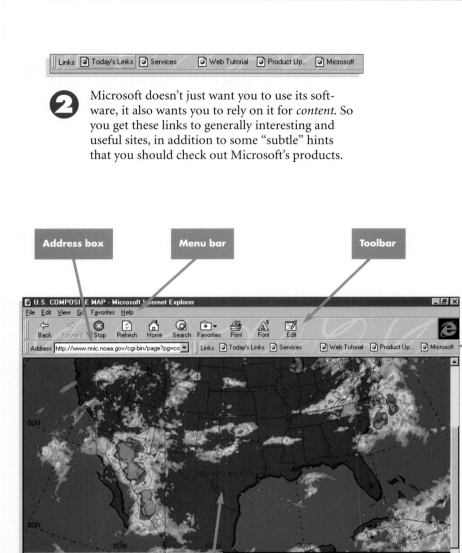

Links bar

4 When you click on any menu item, you'll get a drop-down menu with several options. Note that some of these options have keyboard equivalents, which are often speedier than using the mouse, because they let you bypass the menus.

Web page

5 The Web page is what it's all about. Pretty, isn't it? But there's more to it than meets the screen. Throughout the rest of this book you'll learn what you can do with a Web page aside from gawking and saying "oooh" and "aaaah."

How to Use Toolbar Buttons

O f all the tools Internet Explorer provides you, the toolbar buttons are destined to become the ones you use most often. These buttons duplicate some menu options, but they just take a single click, whereas menu options may require you to click two or three times to get what you want. Most importantly, the toolbar buttons represent the most common actions you'll take while browsing the Web.

Here's a look at these buttons and what they can do for you.

▶ **1** You use the Back button to return to the page you just read.

10 When you grow up (that is, once you make it to Chapter 17), you'll be able to edit Web pages. The Edit button will launch your favorite Web page editor.

9 You can shrink or enlarge Web site text to one of five different configurations by clicking on the Font button. Learn more about it in Chapter 5.

TIP SHEET

▶ **In addition to the Favorites folder, there's a treasure of great sites under Today's Links in the Links bar.**

▶ **The Favorites button is identical to the Favorites menu.**

▶ **Some of the toolbar buttons have keyboard equivalents. For example: Refresh is F5, Stop is Esc, Back is Alt+Left Arrow, and Forward is Alt+Right Arrow.**

2 If you've retraced a site or two, the Forward button can return you to your starting point.

3 Some pages take their sweet time to show up on your screen. If you're impatient or just in a hurry, you can stop the slow download process by clicking on the Stop button.

4 Some sites on the Web are updated once a month, and others get hourly updates, such as news sites. To see if any breaking news happened while you were browsing the current headlines, press Refresh.

5 "Home" is the Web site your browser goes to automatically at the beginning of each session. Once you've started browsing, you can return to your home page by clicking on the Home button.

8 Very often it does make sense to print a page. See "How to Print a Web Page" in Chapter 4 for more information.

7 When Web surfers discover a few sites they like, they want to return to them as often as they can to get their daily fix or to check whether the information has been updated. The Favorites folder keeps links to those sites you're likely to return to. More on this in Chapter 6.

6 Chapter 7 discusses various sites that help you find information on the Web. Chapter 8 explains how to tell Internet Explorer which search site is your favorite one so you can click on the Search button to quickly go to your preferred site.

How to Use the Address Bar

A friend once told me that the only reason he wasn't on the Internet was because of all those "dot coms," as he put it. And he's not alone. Perhaps the most intimidating part of the Internet and the Web are those cryptic URLs. But we're about to demystify these, because, deep down, there's a weird logic to the whole geeky system. Look at the address at the center of the page; it contains several components, and we'll explain each of them. The periods separating the different components are just that: separators.

▶ **1** The *http://* prefix stands for Hypertext Transfer Protocol. This identifies the page or site as adhering to the language of the World Wide Web (Hypertext Markup Language, or HTML), which is discussed in Chapter 17. Other prefixes you'll see are *ftp://* (for file transfer protocol), which is discussed in Chapter 11, and *gopher://*, which is discussed in Chapter 8. Why the ://? To satisfy some obscure techie reason.

TIP SHEET

▶ **Internet Explorer doesn't require that you type the http:// or ftp:// part of an address to go to a site. Instead of http://www.cnet.com, just www.cnet.com will do. Instead of ftp://ftp.winzip.com, ftp.winzip.com will take you there.**

▶ **Looking for a site and don't know its address? If it's a company's site, you can try typing www.*companyname*.com (for example, www.toyota.com). If it's a government agency, try www.*agencyname*.gov; for instance, try www.nasa.gov for NASA.**

▶ **Some URLs are case-sensitive, so pay attention to capital letters in the middle of an address.**

2 *www* stands for World Wide Web, of course. This prefix isn't always used on the Web, but it's very common.

3 *dnai.com* is the domain name, or the name of the host computer where this site is located. The *com* part stands for commercial account, and it's not the only domain name suffix you'll run into. Others include *org* (usually a nonprofit organization), *mil* (military), *gov* (government), *edu* (university or college), and *net* (network). There are also international suffixes, which identify the countries where the hosts are located; these are two-letter abbreviations, such as *jp* for Japan, *il* for Israel, *uk* for United Kingdom, and so on.

http://www.dnai.com/~hubert/new.html

4 *new.html* is the current page. Web pages may have the extensions .html or .htm. Often, you'll see URLs without document names at the end (for example, http://www.dnai.com/~hubert). That means that the document you're looking at is probably named index.html or welcome.html; these are default names that all browsers know to look for. Note that you won't always browse HTML pages. There are a growing number of other types of viewable documents on the Web (such as virtual reality "worlds"), but HTML is the prevalent one.

CHAPTER 4

Getting Started: A Web Cruising Primer

 Submitted for your approval… Jane Webster returns home from work and logs on to the Internet to find information about raising Miniature Schnauzer puppies. "Just for a moment," she promises her unsuspecting husband. She finds several great sites, and those sites provide links to other great sites. Soon, the focus of her search has shifted from dogs to astronomy (it was Leika, that Russian canine astronaut, that caused that detour). From there, she's led onto the righteous path of religion, poetry, gardening, and garbage collection in suburban Illinois. It's 4:00 A.M. She can hear her husband snoring in the bedroom, but she's not tired. She's possessed. She can't stop. She has entered… THE WEB ZONE.

We're about to embark on a truly fantastic voyage. Web browsing is the Great International Pastime. It's books, newspapers, television, movies, and concerts all mixed together, all available at a computer screen near you. Have fun, but don't say I didn't warn you….

How to Go to a Specific Page

Remember URLs? If not, go back to Chapter 3. When you first start out, you'll be typing these quite often. Later, when you've accumulated a collection of Favorites (see Chapter 6), moving around will mostly involve clicking on links. I've created a Web site that we'll use in several exercises, and it will be our first stop. It's a site for book lovers, cleverly disguised as the "Lita Rairee" site. Here it is, at the center of the page.

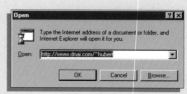

▶ ❶ Select File, Open, and type **http://www.dnai.com/~hubert** in the Open box. Click on OK.

TIP SHEET

▶ **Want to try out a URL you saw in a magazine? Type it exactly as you see it. No spaces are ever allowed, and pay special attention to lower- and uppercase letters.**

▶ **You may be accustomed to the DOS/Windows method of separating directories with backslashes (\), as in c:\hubert\book\ch3. If so, you'll need to get used to the fact that on the Web, only the forward slash is used. Backslashes are still used in addresses that point to files on your hard disk.**

2 Or, click once in the Address box on the tool-bar, type the preceding address over what's in that box, and press Enter. There's no difference between the two methods (that is, they both take you to the same place).

3 You don't really need to type the whole thing. Try typing **www.dnai.com/~hubert** into the Address box; Internet Explorer fills in the http:// prefix for you.

4 Often you'll see addresses that end with a slash (/), such as http://www.dnai.com/~hubert/. In fact, if you click on the down arrow next to the Address box, you'll see that Internet Explorer has recorded all the sites you've visited with trailing slashes. Since Internet Explorer adds the slash to a URL automatically, you can save yourself that extra keystroke.

5 Surprise! You can even browse files on your own hard disk. Say you have a file named topnews.htm in the Daily News folder on your system. To view it in Internet Explorer, just type its full *path* in the address box, as follows: **C:\Daily News\topnews.htm.** Unlike addresses on the World Wide Web, this one isn't case sensitive, so **C:\DAILY NEWS\TOPNEWS.HTM** or **c:\daily news\topnews.htm** would work just the same.

How to Navigate between Pages You've Visited

Internet Explorer knows that once you've visited a site, you may want to return to it. The information is recorded in several places, enabling you to revisit sites using a variety of methods. Whether you want to return to a site one hour later or one week later, you'll be surprised how easy it is.

▶ **1** To go back to the previous page, click on the Back toolbar button or press Ctrl+Left Arrow. (Once you choose Back, the Forward button becomes available; you can use it to reverse your course.) If you'd rather go through a menu, choose Go, Back. You can go back as many pages as you've been through in the current session (that is, since you've launched Internet Explorer).

TIP SHEET

▶ **Links to visited sites are saved in the History Folder as Windows 95 shortcuts on your hard disk. These are tiny files, up to 1K each. But don't let that fool you into thinking you can save thousands of links: Due to some weird quirk, each shortcut takes up anywhere from 4 to 32 times its size, and you can fill up your hard disk in no time if you're not careful. So set a reasonable number of days in the Options dialog box. Also, you can manually remove links from the History folder by deleting their icons.**

▶ **See the next page for information on setting Quick Links to your favorite sites.**

▶ **Read Chapter 6 for information on using the Favorites folder for configuring sites you want to visit again.**

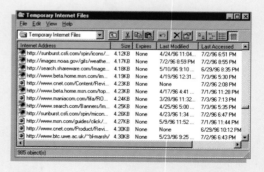

6 Lastly, there's a folder called Temporary Internet Files inside your Windows folder. It contains lots of shortcuts to Web pages, images, and other objects you've checked out on the Net. Open your Windows Explorer, double-click on the Windows folder icon, double-click on Temporary Internet Files, and check it out for links you can't find anywhere else. To launch any of those sites, just double-click on its link.

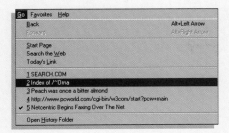

2 Using the Back button (or its opposite, the Forward button), you're driving blindly, never quite knowing which pages you'll hit next. It's OK to use these buttons for a one- or two-page jump, but for more than that, you need more precise tools. Here's one: Under the Go menu, Internet Explorer keeps links to the five sites you've visited most recently, as shown here. Just select Go, and pick one of the five sites from the menu that appears.

3 But you're not limited to five pages (whew). There's a handy History folder, where you'll find hundreds of links to previously visited sites. To go there, select Go, Open History Folder. Find a link you're looking for, and double-click on it to go to that site.

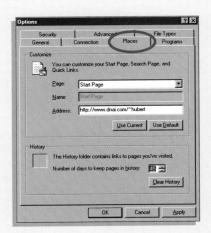

5 You can also click on the down-arrow button next to the Address box on the tool-bar to reveal a list of previously visited sites. Just scroll down, find the one you want and click on it. This selection is not as comprehensive as the History folder, but it's a great shortcut all the same.

4 Don't worry, you won't end up with tens of thousands of links in the History folder. That's useless and fills up your hard disk. Just tell Internet Explorer how many days you want to hold on to links in the History folder, and it'll do its own house cleaning whenever links get too old. To do so, choose View, Options, and click on the Places tab. Click on the up or down arrows next to the number of days to set your preference. The maximum is 1,000 days, but that would be silly. Information on the Net changes so fast that anything older than six months is passé.

How to Set a Start Page and Quick Links

W e're creatures of habit. Every morning we go through the same routine: wash, drink coffee, eat, read the morning paper. So there's no reason to do anything differently when we go Web browsing. If there's a site you like to visit daily, set it as your start (or home) page, so whenever you launch Internet Explorer, you'll go there first. Great candidates for start pages are news sites, where the content is always fresh. So we'll set USA Today as our start page. But check out the Tip Sheet for other suggestions.

▶ **1** Select View, Options, and click on the Places tab. The default start page is the Microsoft Network home page (http://www.msn.com), which should be in the Address box. Select that address with your mouse, and type http://www.usatoday.com over it. Click on OK to close this dialog box.

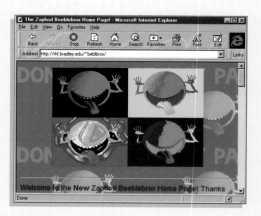

7 Let's test this. Click once on the Don't Panic! button, and you should see this page. If you're a Douglas Adams fan, enjoy your visit. If you're not, repeat steps 4 and 5 but use your favorite site instead.

6 Now your Links bar includes a button labeled Don't Panic!, which you can click on to surf over to the Hitchhiker's Guide to the Galaxy site.

TIP SHEET

▶ **Other suggestions for sites that you may want to consider for your start page are, for general news, CNN at http://www.cnn.com; for sports, ESPNET at http://espnet.sportszone .com; for computer news, c l net at http:// www.cnet.com; for music, MTV at http://mtv.com/; and for business and finance, CNNfn at http://www .cnnfn.com.**

▶ **The ultimate mouse-potato tool, taking you to a different site each time, is Yahoo's Random, at http://random .yahoo.com/bin/ryl.**

2 In a classic case of "you say tomayto and I say tomahto," that start page, when represented on the toolbar, is called home. So even though the USA Today page will open whenever you launch Internet Explorer, you can always return to it quickly by clicking on the Home button.

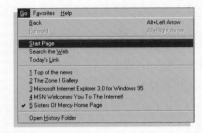

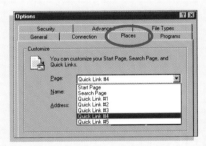

3 And if you need to use the menus (for example, if you've turned off the toolbar as discussed in Chapter 5), select Go, Start Page.

4 You can also override the links on the Links bar and set your own instead, for easy access to frequently visited sites. But whatever you do, take my advice and don't discard to the one labeled Today's Links, because it's chock full of goodies. To assign your own links to any of these five icons, select View, Options, and click on the Places tab. Now click on the down-arrow next to Page, and select a Quick Link you want to replace. For this example, I've selected the third one, because I don't plan on visiting Microsoft's Product Update site that often.

5 Click in the Name box, erase what's there, and type a title for the site you're attaching to this icon. Do you like *Hitchhiker's Guide to the Galaxy* by Douglas Adams? Even if you don't

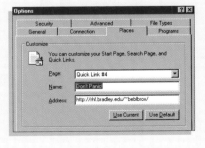

know what it is, trust me on this one…. Type **Don't Panic!** for the title. Then erase the URL in the Address box, type **http://rhf.bradley.edu/~beblbrox/**, and click on OK.

How to Work with Frames

*F*rames are windows-within-windows, so to speak. They are boxes you'll see inside Internet Explorer, which may or may not come with their own scroll bars or visible borders. They're not difficult to operate, but they do need getting used to. Relax, it'll take you all of five minutes to master the art of the frame.

Address http://www.eecis.udel.edu/~markowsk/beatles/

▶ **1** There's a cool Beatles site that I visit periodically (you never know when they're going to re-unite…). Let's go there now. Type **http://www.eecis.udel.edu/~markowsk/beatles** into the Address box and press Enter.

6 Want to resize the frames? Make the right one wider, for example? Move your pointer over the border that separates the frames, until it becomes a double-edged arrow, and then drag to resize.

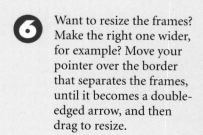

Look at the screen at the center of the page. That Web page has two frames; the left one is the main display, and the right one is just a menu, labeled Contents. When you click on any option on the right,

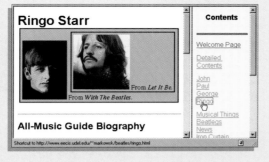

the contents of the frame on the left change. Try clicking on Ringo, and you'll get something that looks like this screen.

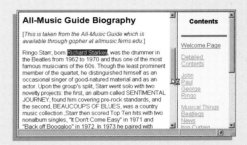

3 You can "browse" each frame independently, using the scroll bar. Try scrolling down the vertical scroll bar on the left pane, and you'll notice that the right frame won't budge.

4 So what happens when you click on the Back button? Only the contents of the left frame change, and the menu on the right stays the same!

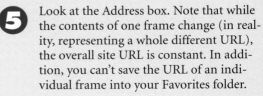

5 Look at the Address box. Note that while the contents of one frame change (in reality, representing a whole different URL), the overall site URL is constant. In addition, you can't save the URL of an individual frame into your Favorites folder.

How to Print a Web Page

The Web is an intellectual democracy, offering research material for elementary school children as well as scholars. When you find a page that you find useful, you may want to save it to your hard disk (see Chapter 6 for more information), or print it so you can give it to a person of the *unwired* persuasion. Here's how you print a Web page.

1 This is a true story: My neighbor needed information about the extraordinary 15th century Dutch painter Hieronimus Bosch. She doesn't have a computer, so she asked me to go online and get some background information for her. I found lots of great sites, and the one she liked the most was at the WebMuseum. It's a long page, and it includes photos of some of Bosch's best known creations. To go there, just type **www.vol.it/wm/paint/auth/bosch** into the Address box and press Enter.

TIP SHEET

▶ **The size and typeface of the printed text is identical to your display. If you've selected extra large fonts (see Chapter 5), the page will print with large fonts, and waste paper. So, regardless of your display preferences, adjust the fonts before you print.**

▶ **Are you curious what those other mysterious codes are, in the Header/Footer dialog box? Here goes: &p stands for page number; &P stands for total number of pages in document: &d stands for date: and &t stands for time.**

2 Before you can print, you may need to change some options, such as margins, paper size, and so on. The wider the margins, the more pages will print. But wide margins give you room for scribbling notes, so let's do that. Select File, Page Setup, and change the right margins to 2.5"—highlight the 0.75" in that box and replace it with **2.5** (no need to type the quotation marks). Click on OK to exit.

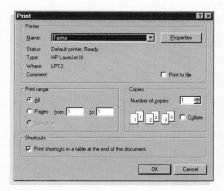

3 Next select File, Print or click on the Print toolbar button. You'll see the Print dialog box. For now, just click on OK to print and see what you get.

4 What's missing on the hard copy? For starters, it doesn't identify its own URL anywhere, only the page title, in the upper-left corner. To fix that, go back to File, Page Setup, and click on the Headers/Footers button. See the &w in the box labeled Upper Left? Replace it with &u. (How's that for the ultimate geekery? *w* is for Web page title, and *u* is for... give up? URL, what else.) Click on OK, and then on the Page Setup's OK.

5 One more thing is missing from the hard copy: all the URLs for the hypertext links, which appear as underlined text. No problem. Click on the Print button again, and click in the check box next to Print Shortcuts in a Table at the End of the Document. When you click on OK, you'll get a very useful printout, complete with all the necessary information.

CHAPTER 5

Configuring the Look of Viewed Pages

The Web is a liberating force, allowing anybody to create and display his or her own pages. The problem is, an artistic flair and a knack for graphic design aren't as common as Web designing is, and most home pages look amateurish (at best). The worst can be headache-inducing.

Fortunately, when you run into a hideous-looking page, you can ask Internet Explorer to override some visual settings, to minimize the impact. In addition, if your vision isn't up to the tiny fonts some "designers" insist on using, you can resize your text to your own comfort level. These and other tricks are what this chapter is about.

How to Change the Fonts in Viewed Pages

What's a pretty font? That's as good a question as, "What's the best kind of music?"—it's all a matter of personal preference. And Internet Explorer lets you set your preference … sometimes. When Web designers force you to view pages in their favorite font, you're pretty much stuck with their settings. Let's visit some sites and see what freedom of choice can mean to your display.

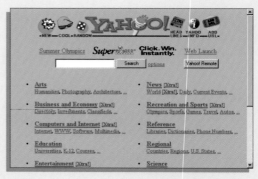

▶ **1** Look at this Yahoo page (http://www.yahoo.com). The text is small, the font isn't easy on the eye, and the colors? *Oy vey!* Fortunately, Yahoo is one of the sites that let you change these settings.

TIP SHEET

▶ You can also set a different font size by selecting View, Fonts, and picking one of the five relative options (Largest, Large, Medium, Small, Smallest).

▶ Use the Smallest font option when you want to see more elements on the screen. Use the Largest option to magnify the contents of the screen; you'll see less information in greater detail.

▶ Department of to-each-her-own: If you like the look of fixed-width fonts (normally, Courier, a typewriter-like typeface), you can choose one as your preferred typeface from the Proportional Font drop-down list in the Options dialog box.

2 To enlarge the font size, click on the Font button on the icon bar. There are five different settings: Normal (the default), Large, Largest, Small, Smallest. You can "cycle" between them by clicking on the Font button repeatedly, until you find your preferred size.

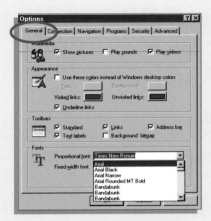

3 Now that the text is more legible, let's fix the typeface. Select View, Options, and click on the drop-down arrow next to Proportional Font. Most TrueType fonts (those that come with Windows) are proportional—an "m" is much wider than an "r," for example. Arial works well for screen display. Try different typefaces from the drop-down list, click on the Apply button, and see how you like the display. When you find a typeface you like, click on OK to exit.

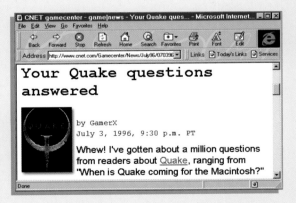

4 This clnet site uses fixed-width (nonproportional) fonts for titles and subtitles. Unfortunately, there's not a whole lot you can do here, because Internet Explorer won't let you select a different font for that screen.

How to Change the Colors of a Page

I keep a jar of aspirin by my keyboard, just in case I run into a Web Page from Hell. You know the type: fluorescent green text over a dizzying purple background with yellow polka dots. Ouch. Internet Explorer lets you override some of those hideous settings, but not all of them. Just as you saw with font selection, some display options are "hard coded" into Web pages, and your only choice is to avoid offensive sites.

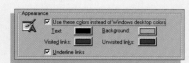

▶ **1** Let's go back to Yahoo's (http://www.yahoo.com). In Chapter 7 you'll find out more about this popular site, so this is a great opportunity to customize it. Yahoo is one of the few sites that let you set your own display options. Choose View, Options, and select the General tab, then click in the check box next to Use These Colors Instead of Windows Desktop Colors.

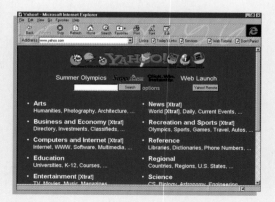

6 If the white background causes screen flicker, which can results in headaches, try reversing the color scheme: Make the background dark and the foreground light. Here's an example.

TIP SHEET

▶ Be prepared to keep changing your color schemes. If, for example, you've set your preferred foreground color to white and you get to a site that has a "hard coded" white background, you won't see anything.

2 First let's select a background. Click on the Background button, and select any color from the palette that pops up. Click on OK to accept that selection.

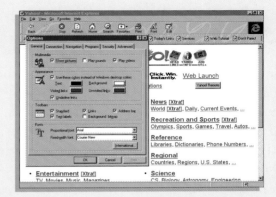

3 Click on Apply and notice the change in the page behind the Options dialog box. If you don't like your selection, click on the Background button again, and try another color. As for me, I selected white, and here's what I got. Don't click on the OK button yet, because you're going to make a few more changes.

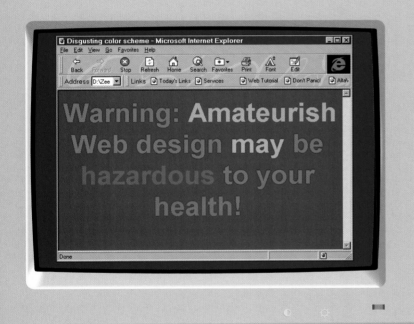

4 Next, click on the button labeled Text, and select any color that pleases you. (But make sure the text contrasts sufficiently with the background so you can still read it!)

5 Finally, set the colors for the hypertext links: one for links you've visited, and another for those you haven't. The reason for this distinction is obvious: You can tell at a glance which sites you've never visited. While you're at it, tell Internet Explorer whether to underline hypertext links. It's easy to see links if they're underlined. On the other hand, too much underlining may make the page look "busy" and unattractive. Make the selection that works best for you. Here's what the Yahoo page looks like after I've set my preferences (notice: no underlining).

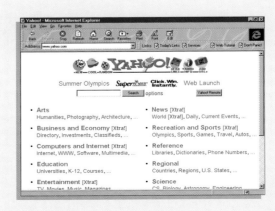

How to Disable/ Enable Other View Options

Look at the Wall Street Journal home page (http://www.wsj.com) in the center of the page. Looks modest and business-like, right? Well, this modesty is deceiving. There are several graphics on that page, and it took Internet Explorer over 20 seconds to "draw" this page on my screen using a regular modem connection, because graphics need to be downloaded before you can see them, and they generally tend to be large. The solution? Disable them. Here's how to do that (and a few other related options).

▶ **1** Go to the WSJ site and note how long it takes to draw. Now select View, Options. Click in the Show Pictures check box to disable the graphics, and click on OK to close the Options dialog box.

TIP SHEET

▶ Some sites are kind enough to give you a Text Only alternative. When you click on it, you get to a lean and mean page, with just the text you want to read. Look for that option at the top of each page you visit.

▶ Internet Explorer saves images from sites you've visited to your hard disk to speed up the process next time you go to those sites. That's called "caching," and although it does make a difference, it doesn't help you with sites that display daily news, with fresh photos posted every day or even several times a day.

2 Now click on the Refresh button and see how fast the page reloads. Almost instantaneously, right? But this time, the page loads without graphics. Internet Explorer displays tiny "placeholders" where graphics are supposed to be.

3 In well-designed pages, you can tell what the missing graphics are all about, because there's a label in their place.

4 Want to see just one graphic (based on its label, perhaps)? Right-click on its icon and select Show Picture. Although the rest of the graphics remain invisible, the one you've picked will be displayed.

5 One last thing: Some sites are so happy to see you, they practically break into song and dance when you visit them. Background music can be amusing when it's a novelty, but it soon becomes highly annoying, if not embarrassing. How would you explain your actions to the boss if you're browsing the Web at the office and your speakers start blasting Heavy Metal music? If you don't use a headset, or if other people's idea of great music doesn't match yours, turn off the Play Sounds option in the Options dialog box.

CHAPTER 6

How to Organize Pages

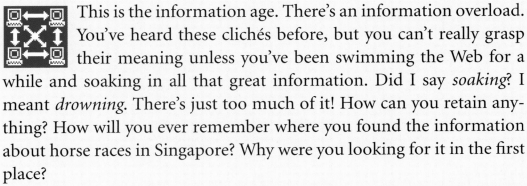 This is the information age. There's an information overload. You've heard these clichés before, but you can't really grasp their meaning unless you've been swimming the Web for a while and soaking in all that great information. Did I say *soaking*? I meant *drowning*. There's just too much of it! How can you retain anything? How will you ever remember where you found the information about horse races in Singapore? Why were you looking for it in the first place?

Luckily, there are ways to handle the flood of information so that you can hold on to what's worth keeping and find it quickly in the future. Chapter 4 discussed different ways of returning to sites you've already visited, using information that Internet Explorer maintains for you. This chapter describes ways of better controlling how information is saved. You'll learn how to use the Favorites folder, how to launch sites from your desktop, and how to save pages and other objects to your hard disk so you can return to them without going online.

How to Use the Favorites Folder

Like millions of others, I was saddened to hear of Ella Fitzgerald's death in June of 1996. Following a few links on the Web, I managed to find lots of great sites dedicated to the First Lady of Song. Because I collect Ella CDs, I knew I needed to keep visiting these sites to find information on new releases of her classics, so I added them to my Favorites folder—a special folder where you keep a list of sites you'd like to return to easily. Here's how.

 1 Type the following URL in the Address box: **http://www.spcc.com/ella/.** You'll get the site shown here.

TIP SHEET

▶ **To select several links to move to a different folder, hold down Ctrl while clicking on the links.**

▶ **If your folders get too cluttered, create folders within folders (these are called *nested folders*).**

▶ **Did you notice the Imported Bookmarks folder in the menu in step 2? It's a sign that I have Netscape's Web browser, Navigator, on my system. Internet Explorer automatically converts Navigator's bookmarks to its own Favorites.**

▶ **Want to have the same set of Favorites at home as you do at work? Just copy the Favorites folder onto a disk and then copy it into the Windows folder on the other system (or send it to yourself via e-mail, as described in Chapter 9).**

▶ **For a quick Add to Favorite, try Ctrl+D. You'll bypass the dialog box asking you to name the site.**

9 Now click on any link to a music-related site and click on the Move button. In the dialog box that appears, double-click on the folder you want to move the link to and click on OK. Repeat the process for other topics you want to move. When you're done, your Favorites menu will be organized in a more logical fashion.

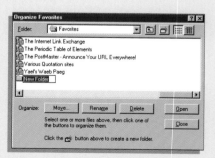

8 A new folder icon labeled New Folder appears. Type a new label, such as **Music**, over the existing one.

2 To save this site to your Favorites folder, choose Favorites, Add To Favorites.

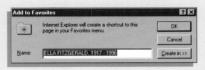

3 The Add to Favorites dialog box lets you name the link, or accept the page's title as a label. For now, click on OK to accept that title.

4 Next time you pull down the Favorites menu, the page you choose (the Ella page, in this case) will be there. You can then go to the site by clicking on that entry.

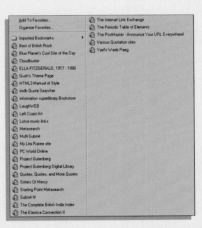

5 I regularly add sites to my Favorites folder, and if you're like me, pretty soon you'll have a Favorites menu with too many entries. Although the sites are sorted alphabetically, the menu shown here is still a mess, which defeats the purpose of the Favorites menu. You need some order here.

7 You can group most of these links by topic: news, music, computers, personal, art, and so on. First you need to create a folder for each category. Start by clicking on the Create New Folder button.

6 To organize this mess, select Favorites, Organize Favorites. You'll see the Organize Favorites dialog box.

How to Launch Sites from Your Desktop

The Favorites menu is very useful, but you need to be in Internet Explorer to open it, which means going through your designated start page—an unnecessary detour. You can launch Internet Explorer quickly by clicking on a shortcut to a site. Where can you find these shortcuts? The links in the Favorites folder are shortcuts, but they're buried deep inside two or three levels of your hard-disk structure. Your desktop is much more accessible, so here you'll learn how to use it as a launch pad.

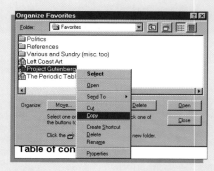

 1 Let's start with the Favorites menu. See something you'd like to put on the desktop? No problem. Select Favorites, Organize Favorites. Now right-click on any icon you want to save to the desktop and select Copy. Click on Close to exit the Organize Favorites dialog box.

TIP SHEET

▶ **You can also send these shortcuts to others via e-mail. Right-click on any shortcut, choose Send To, and then choose Internet Mail Recipient. The e-mail program will launch with that icon as an attachment. See Chapter 9 for information about what to do next.**

▶ **The desktop isn't the only place where you can save these shortcuts, of course. Any folder on your hard disk will do, as long as you know how to get to it quickly.**

2 Right-click on any unoccupied area on the taskbar, and select Minimize All Windows. Then right-click anywhere on the desktop and choose Paste to copy the shortcut to the desktop.

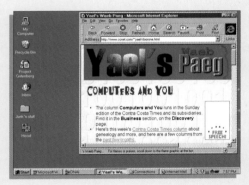

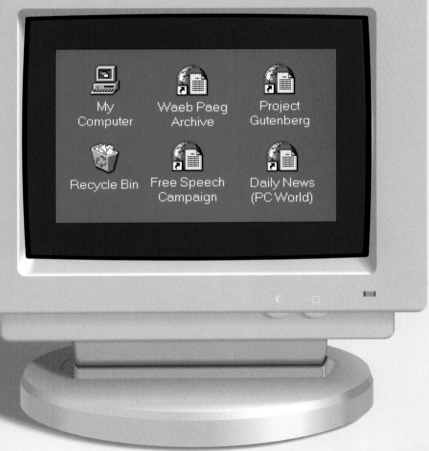

3 A more elegant way to do this is to drag a link directly from a Web page to the desktop. To do this, first make sure the Internet Explorer window doesn't fill the screen. (Click on the Restore button.)

4 See a link you want to save? Drag it to the desktop and drop it anywhere you like. While you're dragging, your pointer will change to the standard Windows 95 pointer for dragging.

6 Now right-click anywhere on the desktop and choose Paste Shortcut.

5 If you don't like dragging, you can right-click on a link (whether it's a text or an image) and select Copy Shortcut.

How to Save Pages and Other Objects to Your Hard Disk

S aving links to URLs is fine if you want to return to them at the drop of a hat. But some information—famous speeches, books, and so on—never changes, and those pages should reside on your hard disk so you don't have to log on whenever you need to look at them. Doing some research on Shakespeare's sonnets? Find them online and save them to your system. Whenever you need to look at that document, just double-click on its icon, and Internet Explorer launches, letting you review the contents without going online.

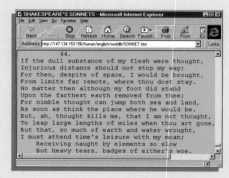

▶ **1** You can find Shakespeare's sonnets 1 through 45 at http://147.134.153.156/ human/english/worldlit/SONNET.htm.

TIP SHEET

▶ **To read saved files, just select File, Open, Browse, locate the file you want to read, and click on OK.**

▶ **To convert HTML files to a format your word processor can understand, open them in your word processor (note: only Windows 95 word processors understand HTML) and select File, Save As to save the file in any format other than HTML.**

2 Choose File, Save As File.

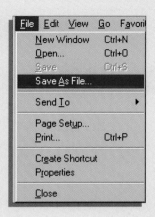

3 In the Save As dialog box, click on the drop-down arrow next to the Save In box, and choose the drive and folder where you want to place the file.

4 When you get to that folder, type a name for the file (Shakespeare's Sonnets would be good), and click on Save.

5 You can also save a file without actually going to its site. If you see a link to a file you want to save, right-click on it, and choose Save Target As.

6 Internet Explorer starts downloading the file to your hard disk, and then pauses to ask you where the file belongs. Once again, click on the drop-down arrow next to the Save In box, find the right folder, and click on Save.

TRY IT!

Given time, finding your favorite things on the Web is easy. In this Try It, you'll have a chance to use the skills you've learned up to this point to navigate the Web with Internet Explorer and then save your favorite sites for future visits. Then, before your Favorites folder becomes too cluttered to be of use, you'll practice organizing your favorites, creating multiple folders and moving favorite sites between these folders. Whether you're an "everything in its place, and a place for everything" neat freak, or an "I'll get to it tomorrow" slob, keeping your favorites in order makes for a better Web surfing experience.

Address | http://www.dnai.com/~hubert/

Let's start at the Lita Rairee site. Click in the Address box on the toolbar and type **www.dnai.com/~hubert**. Then press Enter.

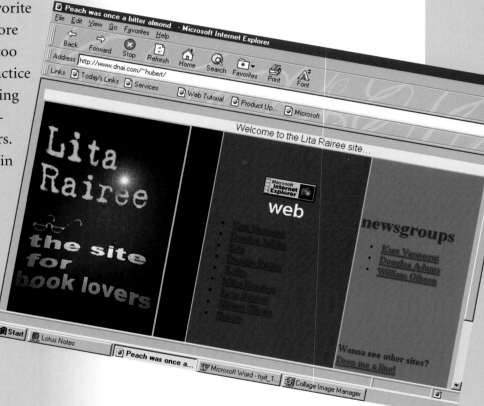

Click once again in the Address box and enter **www.cnet.com**; then press Enter. Let's add this site to your Favorites folder.

Click on the Favorites toolbar button. This drops down a menu with two choices—Add to Favorites and Organize Favorites. Click once on Add to Favorites.

Accept the default page name of Welcome to CNET Online by clicking on the OK button.

Now click on the Favorites toolbar button. You'll notice that the Welcome to CNET Online link has been added to your Favorites list. Let's continue to add sites to your Favorites list; later we'll organize them into different folders.

Let's surf over to the PC Computing three-in-one Web site for more technology news and reviews. Click in the Address box, type **www.pccomputing.com**, and press Enter.

Right-click on a blank space on the PC Computing page to open the menu shown here. Scroll down and click on Add To Favorites.

The Add to Favorites box opens showing the default name of the page—PC Computing Choice Page.

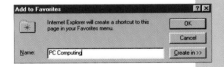

Let's rename this favorite. Since the text is already selected, simply type **PC Computing** and either click on the OK button or press Enter.

Continue to next page ▶

TRY IT!

Continue below

10

Click in the Address box, type **www.well .com/user/ lawsuit**, and press Enter. Choose Add to Favorites from the Favorites menu or from the context menu that opens when you right-click. (Lawsuit is a San Francisco–based 10-piece band powered by an incredible horn and rhythm section.)

11

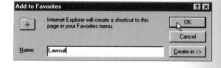

With the default name of the site highlighted in the Add to Favorites box, type **Lawsuit** and then press Enter or click on the OK button to add the Lawsuit site to Favorites.

12

Add the pages at **www.warnerbros.com** and **www.fox.com** to your Favorites list by whichever method you prefer. Accept the default names for the pages.

13

Click on the Favorites toolbar button to see your five favorites organized alphabetically on the pull-down menu.

14

To organize the five sites saved in your Favorites folder, click on the Favorites button in the toolbar and then choose Organize Favorites.

15

In the Organize Favorites box, click on the Create New Folder button.

16

You'll now see a new folder named New Folder in your Favorites box. Type **Computing** and then press Enter.

17

Click on the PC Computing favorite to select it, then click on the Move button.

18

In the Browse for Folder box, click on the Computing folder you just created, then click on the OK button. Follow these exact same steps for the clnet online site. You should now have two sites in your Computing folder.

19

Now let's create an Entertainment folder. Just as in step 15, click on the Create New Folder button.

20

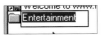

Type **Entertainment** to replace the New Folder label and press Enter.

21

Click on the Warner Bros. favorite, then while holding down the Shift key, click on the www.fox favorite. Then click on the Move button.

22

Click on the Entertainment folder then on the OK button to move the sites into Entertainment.

23

Move the mouse pointer over the Lawsuit favorite, then press and hold down the mouse button while you drag it to the Entertainment folder. Release the mouse button to drop the favorite in the folder.

24

Click on the Close button to close the Organize Favorites box.

CHAPTER 7

Finding Information
on the Internet

 Contrary to what you've been told all your life, finding a needle in a haystack isn't an impossible task—if you have the right tool. Although the Internet is huge and ever-expanding, finding just the information you want is surprisingly easy.

There are two types of search tools on the Net: search engines and directories. *Search engines* are programs that find information based on *keywords.* For example, if you're looking for the names of all current U.S. senators, you can search for the words "senate" or "senators." The search engine then looks for documents on the Net that contains your keyword. In contrast, *directories* examine various sites, and then evaluate and categorize them. You can find information in a directory by browsing its categories and reading brief descriptions of the sites. In some directories, senators are likely to found under the headings Government/Legislative Branch.

There are advantages to both types of search tools. For quick-and-dirty searches, you can't beat a search engine. But if you're looking for suggestions, directories are chock-full of those because they are maintained by humans. In contrast, search engines operate without human intervention, using computer programs to find what you're looking for. So let's dive into this virtual stack of hay and find some real gems.

How to Use Yahoo!

Yahoo! is one of the most popular sites on the Net. It's the granddaddy of all directories, and for a good reason. There are incredible volumes of information on Yahoo!, all organized in an easy-to-navigate hierarchical system. (In fact, Yahoo! stands for *Yet Another Hierarchical Officious Oracle*, after the Oracle database on which it's based.) Are you a star gazer? We're going to look for comets.

TIP SHEET

- ▶ **Yahoo! is not only for people who know what they want. You can visit lots of exciting new sites by clicking on the New, Cool, and Random buttons next to the Yahoo! logo on Yahoo's home page. This is the ultimate channel-surfing.**

- ▶ **If you're going to return to a Yahoo! area in the future, better add it to your Favorite Places. For example, to check out new Hyakutake photos in the future, click on the Add to Favorites button after step 6. This will add a shortcut to the URL http://search.yahoo.com/bin/search? p=hyakutake+photo to your Favorite Places folder. See Chapter 6 for information about Favorite Places.**

- ▶ **If your keyword search yields no matches, Yahoo! can pass your query on to other search sites on the Net. Note the line at the bottom of the screen that points to "Other Search Engines," and try each of them until you find what you're looking for.**

▶ **1** Type the address **www.yahoo.com** in the Address box. This will take you to Yahoo!'s home page, shown in the middle of this page.

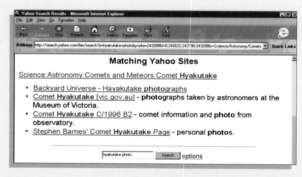

6 If you're looking for photos of the comet, your search should be more specific. Just type **hyakutake photo** in the Search box and click on the Search button. (You don't need to worry about using uppercase or lowercase letters—it's all the same to Yahoo!.) That instructs Yahoo! to present only matches that contain both these words. The resulting list shows your search words in boldface.

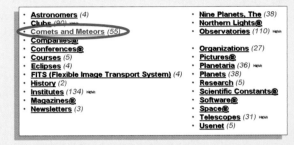

2 Click on Science. The resulting page is full of subcategories within the Science category. The number next to each subcategory refers to the number of entries in it. Click on Astronomy.

3 See the Comets and Meteors entry? Click on it.

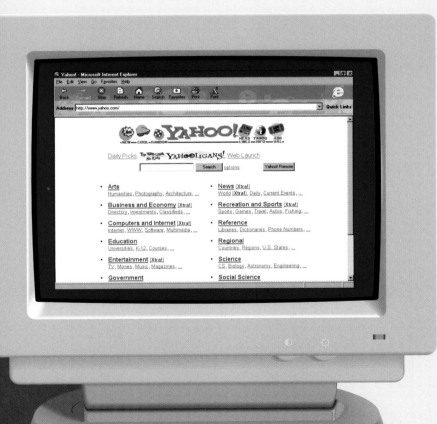

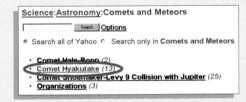

4 Back in March 1996, Comet Hyakutake was a spectacular event. If you missed it, you can select that entry now and browse among the various sites and documents listed here.

5 Are you all clicked out? There's actually an easier way to get what you want. If you know what you're looking for (including the correct spelling of Hyakutake), there's an easier way. On Yahoo!'s home page or any subsequent pages, just type **hyakutake** in the Search box and click on the Search button.

How to Use Open Text

The Open Text software company makes the Open Text search engine, which is based on full-text indexing of millions of Web pages and other documents on the Net. A *full-text index* ensures that every word or number in a document can be searchable. For example, look for "oz" and you'll get hundreds of matches: the Wizard of Oz, Australian sites (the two-letter abbreviation for Australian sites is "oz"), and so on. Luckily, Open Text lets you be as specific as you want, so you can narrow down the result of your query to a manageable size. Open Text presents the matches as a numbered list, where each entry includes a link to an Internet document, plus the first few lines from that document, plus two very handy options: You can go directly to the place in the document that contains the match, or you can be directed to other documents on the Net that contain related information.

Ready? We're going to collect as much information as we can about The Cranberries—the Irish band, not the Thanksgiving condiment.

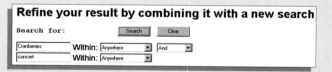

1 Log on to the Open Text search site by typing **www.opentext.com/ omw/f-omw.html** in the Address box.

6 Now you can mix and match different search conditions, such as And, Or, and so on. Combining two searches with And may narrow down the search, while using Or may broaden it. For example, *Cranberries And concert* will find any match that contains both words. *Cranberries Or concert* will find all the matches that contain either word, which is probably not what you want in this case. You can also specify where the keywords should appear: anywhere in the document, in the title, in the URL, or in the summary. Click on the drop-down arrow next to the box labeled Within, select Summary, make sure that And is selected, and type **concert** in the Search box below. Click on the Search button, and you can be pretty confident that you won't get too many recipes....

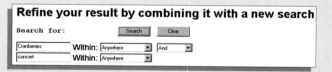

TIP SHEET

▶ **Because Open Text indexes millions of documents, be very precise when you type a keyword, or you may get thousands of matches, most of which are irrelevant to your search. For example, if you're looking for travel information for Australia, don't type "au," because you'll get every Ozzie site known to Open Text, plus thousands of audio files. A better way would be to combine Australia with *tourism*.**

▶ **Use the But Not option to exclude unwanted elements. For example, to look for information about yogurt cultures (the microscopic ones, not Berkeley in the Sixties), combine yogurt with *But Not frozen*.**

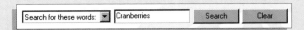

2 See the box to the left of the Search button? Type **Cranberries** in this box and click on Search.

3 It seems we've hit the jackpot. 880 matches! Scroll down the page to get a first look at the list.

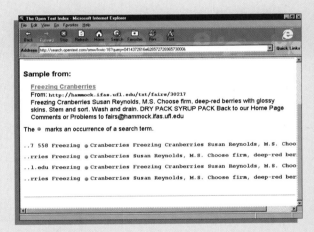

4 What's that? Freezing Cranberries? Must be very cold in Ireland, or we're looking at pages about the fruit, not the band. Just to be sure, click on See Matches on the Page. All matches are labeled with red bullets. Mystery solved; some of these matches are recipes.

5 But you were looking for the band Cranberries, and you want to find out when they're coming to your neck of the woods. Click on the Back button on the toolbar, scroll to the top of the page, and click on "Improve your result."

How to Use AltaVista

One of the most powerful and comprehensive search sites on the Net is AltaVista. This is not a structured directory à la Yahoo!, but odds are, if you're looking for practically *anything*, AltaVista will find it. There's a price to be paid, though: AltaVista was clearly designed by computer geeks who think the whole world speaks the same awkward language they obviously revel in. This means that you need to type in things that aren't always English, but fear not, it's all rather simple, and the online help is terrific. AltaVista's greatest advantage is that you can search for nontext parts of Web pages, such as embedded images and page titles. This is not limited to the Web. You can also search on newsgroups and practically anything that's on the Internet. I need a graphic of a baby for a report I'm working on. Let's see how easy it is to find.

TIP SHEET

▶ Curious to find out how many people link to your site? Type link:www.*yoursite*.com in the Search box. For example, type link:www.pcworld.com to find out how many Web pages link to *PC World* magazine's site.

▶ There's more to AltaVista than meets the eye. To master all the gems this search engine provides, click on Help in the logo, and read or print the resulting document.

▶ You can easily end up with 30,000 matches, or "hits," if you're not careful, so use the minus and plus signs to be more specific. Here's how: To specify that you're looking for Java, the island, not the Internet programming language, type java -internet +travel. In AltaVista's lingo, the plus sign is the same as And in other search engines. The minus is the equivalent of But Not or Except For.

▶ **1** Type **www.altavista.com** in the Address box. This will take you to AltaVista's home page. From there, click on the Search Engine button, which takes you to the screen shown in the center of this page.

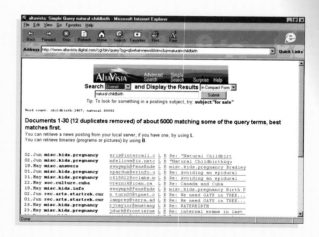

6 On to the next quest. Let's look for information about natural childbirth. In the Search box, type **natural childbirth**. Click on the down-arrow next to Search, and select Newsgroups. Click on the Submit button, and here's everything people have to say about the subject.

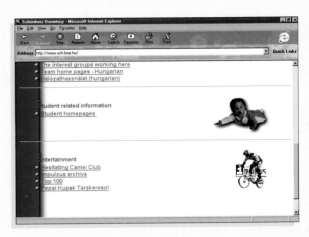

2 In the Search box, type
image:baby. This tells AltaVista
that you're looking for a graphic
with the word "baby" in its name.
Click on the Submit button. A few
seconds later, you'll get a screen
with lots of listings.

3 What have you got to lose? Click on the first
match in that list. When I did that, it gave me a
page in Hungarian. That's okay, because I'm
looking for a baby, and there it is, at the bottom
of the page. It's a cute one, all right, but I don't
want a photo, so I'll go back and check out the
other 5,000 matches....

4 Click on the Back toolbar button
and look at the list again. With a
large number of matches, it
makes more sense to have one
entry per line. Click on the
down-arrow button to the right
of Display the Results and select
In Compact Form.

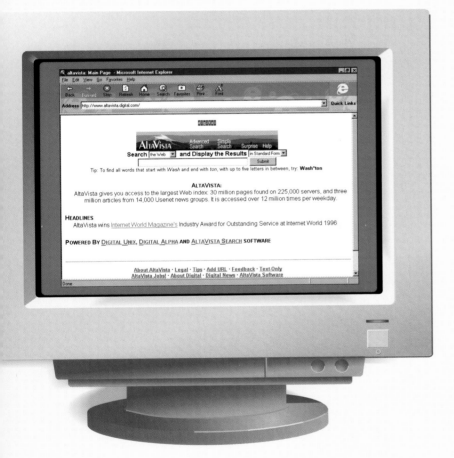

5 Click on the Submit button to regenerate the list.
Now, that's more like it. Each match takes up one line,
and you're looking at a list of ten matches. Where are
all the others? See the 1 through 20 list at the bottom
of the screen? Each number represents a different
page, each holding 10 matches. You can click on those
numbers in sequence or randomly. When you click on
Next, you'll go to yet another group of 20 pages.

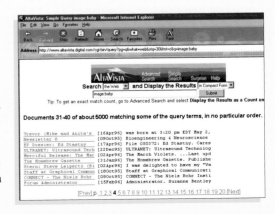

How to Use Infoseek

Like Yahoo!, Infoseek is a structured directory. Beyond categorized listings, it features several unique search options that make it a valuable addition to anybody's search tool arsenal. Let's check it out. This time we're looking for information about David Letterman and the Late Show.

▶ Although you can type all your search items in lowercase, use uppercase when you want to distinguish a word as a proper name. For example, "Cypress Hill" is more likely to take you to a place with that name than "cypress hill," which will result in all kinds of documents about trees and landscape.

▶ Infoseek lets you set up a customized page with links to information that's important to you. Type http://personal.infoseek.com to create your Personal Page, complete with personal news, e-mail addresses, stock quotes, and even street maps.

▶ For links to news items and magazine articles, click on the iZone button on Infoseek's home page. Here you'll find great information from *U.S. News*, *PC World*, and *Bon Appétit*, to name but a few.

▶ ❶ Type **www.infoseek.com** in the Address box. This will take you to Yahoo!'s home page, shown in the center of this page.

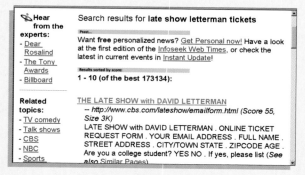

❻ So how easy is it to get tickets for the Late Show? Let's find out. Click on the Infoseek Guide button at the top of the page to return to Infoseek's home page. Type **late show letterman tickets** in the Search box, and you're on your way to the Big Apple (well…close enough).

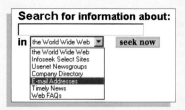

2 On the left you see the categories in the directory. Next to the Seek Now button it currently says In World Wide Web. Click on the drop-down arrow to see more options, and select E-mail Addresses.

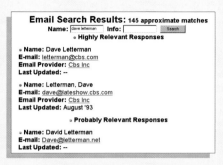

3 Type **dave letterman** in the Search box and click on the Seek Now button. What do you know; the man has lots of e-mail addresses. But does he?

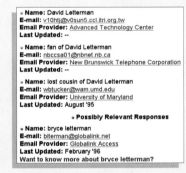

4 Actually, only a couple of those addresses belong to the Most Powerful Man in Show Business. The rest are other David Lettermans, including some that just sound close enough.

5 Want to narrow it down to the pencil-thrower? Scroll to the top of the page, and type **cbs** in the Info box. That tells Infoseek that you want to limit your search to any David Letterman who works at CBS.

CHAPTER 8

Advanced Searches

 The ease with which you can find information on the Internet has its disadvantages. The most common headache is the volume of data you get whenever you search for anything. It's not unusual to get 2,000 "hits" for a simple query, either because your search terms are too broad, or because there's just too much of what you're looking for. Fortunately, there are some programs that help you streamline your search: shareware.com helps you find software on the Net, Four11 lets you find people on the Net, and search.com helps you find a search engine that's right for you.

To get the best search results, avoid general terms: *love, drugs, war, computers, literature.* Instead, use specific terms. For example, instead of looking for *love,* search for "single bars AND Atlanta" or "matchmaker AND San Francisco."

For a more focused search, first try your luck in the directories (Yahoo, InfoSeek, and so on). They tend to separate the wheat from the chaff. For example, when I entered **personal computer** into Yahoo's search box, I got back about 500 hits, most of them appropriate.

You can also check out specialized ("vertical") search sites. For example, you'll get fewer—and more accurate—hits when you look for computer prices on clnet's Product Finder or on *PC World*'s interactive Buyer's Guide than on an all-purpose site such as InfoSeek or Lycos.

How to Use shareware.com to Search for Software

One of the great things about the Internet is the free and inexpensive software that you can download and test drive before you buy. Shareware, or trialware, lets users experiment with the software before they pay. Some programs come with no strings attached, and it's up to you, the scrupulous consumer, to pay a registration fee if you decide to keep using them. Other programs contain "time bombs" that cause them to expire sometime after you've downloaded them. And freeware, as its name indicates, is the most generous of all. My favorite shareware site on the Net is shareware.com, a site run and operated by c|net.

1 Type **http://www.shareware.com** into the Address box and press Enter. The shareware.com site appears.

6 Once you click on a site, Internet Explorer starts downloading the file. When it's done, it asks you where on your hard disk you want to save it; or, if you have an "unzip" utility, it unzips the file so you can proceed with the installation.

TIP SHEET

▸ **See Chapter 11 for more information on downloading and installing shareware and freeware programs.**

▸ **Don't know where to start? Check out the "Newest" and "Most popular" sections on the shareware.com home page.**

2 The hottest game in the history of the universe is Doom, and now there's Quake, a new game from the same company (id Software). Let's see how easy it is to find it. Type **Quake** in the Quick Search box and click on the Search button.

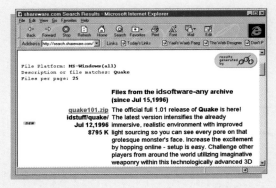

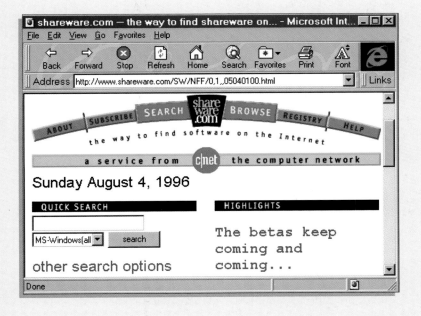

3 The next screen shows the matches (there could be more than one quake, other than a game). Read the brief description to make sure that you have the right file, and then click on the file name's hyperlink (in this example, quake101.zip).

4 shareware.com sends you to a listing of sites all over the world where you can find that file. Note the "ratings" next to each location. These indicate the likelihood that you'll make a successful attempt to connect to that site. Five squares give you a 80 to 100 percent success rate. Generally speaking, you want to select a site in your country, but the rating system is very reliable in predicting the level of success. Click on any of the sites to start downloading.

5 If you'd rather check approximately how long it'll take you to download before you make your move, scroll down to the bottom of the page, until you see a screen something like this.

How to Use Four11 to Search for People

There are millions of people on the Internet. The exact number is hard to pinpoint, as the Net grows at an amazing rate. Wouldn't it be nice to find anybody who has an e-mail account? Don't get excited, because it's next to impossible. There are several "white pages" directories, but they only contain a fraction of the addresses—basically only people and organizations who have released their data to the directories. My favorite one is Four11, which has a good-size listing and an easy-to-use interface. To demonstrate how easy it is, I'm going to look for some old high school friends. (Did I say "old"? I meant long-forgotten.)

▶ **1** Type **http://www.four11.com** into the Address box and press Enter.

7 The e-mail program launches; I type my message and send it. Mission accomplished.

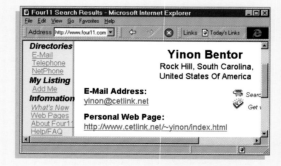

6 Now I know where they live, too. Hey, the kid has his own Web page! I'll check it out later. Right now, I'll click on his e-mail address to send a message to his mother.

2 Type the first and last name of the person you're looking for and then click on the Search E-Mail button. Here I typed **Orna** into the First Name field and **Bentor** into the Last Name one.

3 Internet Explorer warns you that you're about to send what amounts to be personal information over the Internet, making yourself vulnerable to all kinds of snoops. Click on Yes; you needn't be too concerned at this point.

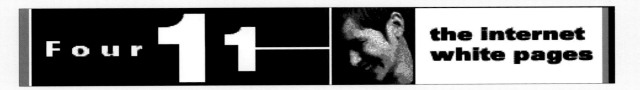

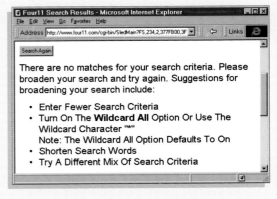

4 No luck. Well, not all is lost. I click on Search Again (or on the Back button on the toolbar) and try a different route (this time, just the last name).

5 Success! My friend may not have an e-mail account, but her husband and son do. I'll click on her son's name to discover more information about him.

How to Use search.com

The proliferation of Internet search engines is dizzying. There are hundreds, if not thousands, of bona fide search sites all over the world, some catering to the general population, others with a limited "niche." As soon as you start searching for information on the Net, you'll come to a realization that you need a search engine to locate all the search engines. And fortunately, someone has already thought of it. It's called search.com, and it's the Grand Central Station of all search sites.

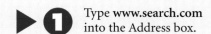

1 Type www.search.com into the Address box.

TIP SHEET

▶ Use the Personalize option on search.com to create your very own search page with links to search engines or categories you're likely to revisit often.

▶ Click on the A-Z List option to see the whole list (alphabetized, but not categorized) of the search engines on search.com.

▶ Another great all-in-one search site is Starting Point (http://www.stpt.com/).

2 The screen you see at the center of the page comes up. There are two "panes" here: The right one gives you a few major search sites to get you started, and the left one has everything you'd ever need (more on that in a moment).

3 The left pane lists search categories, from Arts to Automotive to Lifestyle to Science and so on. Click on any category to find search engines relevant to that topic. I'm looking for information about insomnia, so I'll try Health.

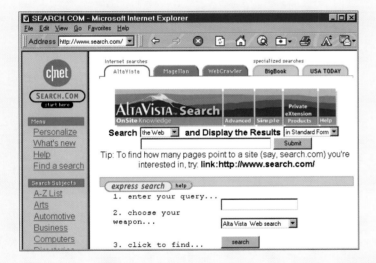

4 Here's just a sampling of the health-related search sites.

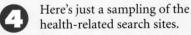

5 Mental Health Net sounds like the right place to start, so let's click on it to find out more. I won't bore you with the details, but the bottom line is, I haven't been sleeping lately. The cure, as I've discovered in my relentless scientific research, is *to finish this book.*

CHAPTER 9

Using the Internet Mail Software

The word "mail" used to trigger a deep sense of guilt in me. All those people I never wrote back to, all the friends with whom I'd lost touch, all because sending a letter was nothing short of a chore. The writing itself wasn't a problem, but finding envelopes and stamps and remembering to leave the letters out for the letter carrier was enough to turn me into a procrastinator with a huge guilt complex.

And then there was e-mail. Now I reply to messages within minutes of receiving them, I've renewed old friendships, and I haven't had to buy stamps in years.

Internet Mail is a program that comes with the Internet Explorer (or separately). It serves as your envelope and stamp, and the Internet is your letter carrier. The best part is, what used to take two days or longer to deliver, now takes a few minutes. No hail, no sleet, no snow.

So quit licking stamps for a moment, because we're about to learn how to configure Internet Mail and then use it to send and receive e-mail.

Installing and Setting Up Internet Mail

If you don't have Internet Mail yet, you need to go to the Microsoft Web site and download it. Note that this will get you both Internet Mail and Internet News (which you'll need for Chapter 10). If Internet Mail is already installed on your system, skip steps 1 and 2. Before you can start using Internet Mail, you need to set it up, so it knows who you are and what your e-mail address is.

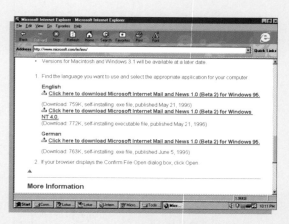

▶ **1** Type **www.microsoft.com/ie/imn** in the Address box to go to Microsoft's Internet Explorer/Internet Mail and News Web page. Scroll down the page until you see the link for downloading Internet Mail and News. Select your version of Windows, and the download process will start.

TIP SHEET

▶ **Do you get a lot of e-mail every day? You can automate message retrieval by selecting the Read tab in the Options dialog box. Make your selection in the Check for New Message Every box. The program will dial and send/receive messages at scheduled intervals, in the background, while you're doing other things.**

▶ **Add Internet Mail to your desktop by opening My Computer, using the right mouse button to drag the Internet Mail icon onto the desktop, and choosing Create Shortcut Here.**

▶ **The Spy versus Spy tip: The name you type in the Options dialog box doesn't necessarily have to be your full (or real) name. It can be any name you want your recipients to see.**

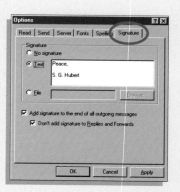

6 Do you always sign your messages the same way? You can tell Internet Mail to do it for you, automatically. Click on the Signature tab, choose the Text option, and type any letter closing you like. Click on OK when you're done.

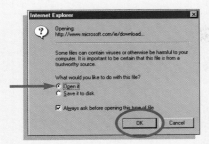

2 You'll see a dialog box asking whether you want to save or open that file. If you choose Save to Disk, you'll later need to select the file and run the installation. An easier way is to choose Open It, which will run the installation module for you as soon as you download the file. When the installation is complete, the appropriate icons are added to My Computer.

3 To launch Internet Mail, double-click on My Computer, and then on the Internet Mail icon.

4 Before you can start using Internet Mail, you need to tell it who you are and how you want to use the program. Choose Mail from the menu bar, and then click on Options. You'll see this dialog box full of options.

5 First you need to enter your personal data. To do so, click on the Server tab in the Options dialog box. Enter your name in the Name box and your e-mail address in the E-mail Address box. You'll need to get the information for the outgoing and incoming mail from your Internet service provider. Type your user ID with that provider in the POP3 Account box, and then type your password in the Password box.

How to Customize Internet Mail

Like any other software, Internet Mail can be customized to look and behave the way you want it to. For example, if you don't like the icons at the top, you can put them somewhere else. Fonts too small? Make them larger. These factory-set options (called *defaults* in computer lingo) are easy to change.

▶ **1** If you've closed Internet Mail, launch it again from My Computer. There are several elements to this window; check out the screen in the center of this page to become familiar with them.

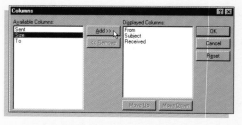

8 Lastly, you may want to include information about the size of messages. To do so, choose View, Columns. Click on the word Size on the left pane, click on Add, and the Size column is added to your display.

7 If you want to see more text on the screen at once, you can get rid of several items that take up too much real estate on your screen. Choose View, and then choose Toolbar to remove the toolbar from the window. Again, choose View, Icon Bar. Repeat the process for Status Bar. You've trimmed the frames of this window quite a bit and gained extra viewing space. The last thing you can remove is the header information bar; do it by choosing View, Preview Pane, and then choosing Header Information. You can reverse any of these steps any time you want.

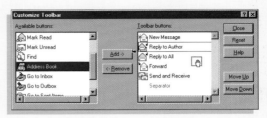

2 Let's start with the icon bar. Would you like it better if it were on the left side? No problem. Right-click anywhere in the icon bar, and choose Left.

3 You can easily add icons to the icon bar (or remove those you don't need). Right-click anywhere within the icon bar and choose Customize Toolbar. To add Address Book to the icon bar, for example, just drag its icon from the left pane (Available buttons) to the right one (Toolbar buttons). (Your pointer will appear as a hand over a square.) Drop the button where you want it to appear in relation to the other icons. To remove an icon from the icon bar, just drag it from the right pane to the left one.

Folder Box   **Menu bar**   **Tool bar**   **Icon bar**

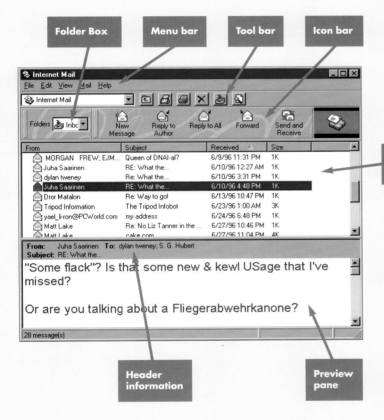

Message pane

Header information

Preview pane

4 The icon bar and the Folders box are resizable. See for yourself: Move your pointer over the left border of the icon bar (the one that looks like two lines), and when your pointer changes into a double-headed arrow, drag it right or left until you're happy with the results.

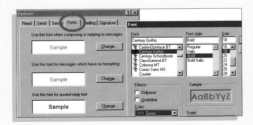

6 And what's with those tiny fonts? If you're squinting at the screen, thinking they should have sent you a magnifying glass with the software, here's your re-lief: Choose Mail, Options, and then click on the Fonts tab. Click on the top Change button and make your selection (typeface, color, and size). Click on OK to save this option, and repeat the process for the other two Change buttons.

5 The Internet Mail screen is divided into two panes: The top one shows a list of messages, and the bottom one displays the contents of the currently selected message. Don't like the way it looks? You can align the panes side by side. Just choose View, Preview Pane, and then Split Vertically.

How to Create and Send an E-Mail Message

D*ear Tooth Fairy,*
    Last month I left a tooth under my pillow,
but I think you didn't know about it, because you
never came, and the next day my baby sister stole
the tooth and gave it to the dog. This time I'm not
taking any chances. I'm sending you this e-mail to
let you know that a brand new tooth is waiting for
you tonight under my pillow, so please don't forget
to come and leave me two dollars. One for last
time, and one for today.
    Sincerely,
Jesse from Peachtree Court

TIP SHEET

▶ **Time, as you well know, is money. Do as much**
   as you can off line, and you'll minimize your
   connect charges. When you're done composing
   several messages, click on the Send and Receive
   icon on the icon bar, and the program will dial
   your Internet service provider and send those
   messages in one fell swoop.

▶ **Your messages are saved in the Outbox folder**
   until they're sent. If you change your mind and
   don't want to send that Dear John letter after
   all, click on the down arrow to the left of the
   Inbox icon, choose Outbox, click on the mes-
   sage you want to delete, and then press the
   Delete key on your keyboard.

▶ **If you use a lot of acronyms in your messages,**
   tell the spell checker to ignore them: Choose
   Message, Options, click on the Spelling tab, and
   then check the option Words in Uppercase.

▶ **Many Web pages have links to e-mail ad-**
   dresses. When you click on such a link (usually
   identified as "Drop me a line," or something
   similar), you'll launch Internet Mail, complete
   with your signature and your return address.

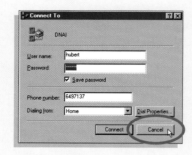

▶ **1** To start writing a message, first launch Internet Mail. If you get the Connect To dialog box, click on the Cancel button, because you're not ready to go on line yet.

2 Click on the New Message icon in the icon bar.

3 Click anywhere in the To box and type the e-mail address of the recipient. Then click anywhere in the Subject box and type a brief subject for this message.

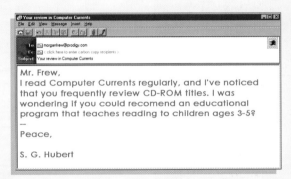

4 Type your message in the bottom pane. Can't spel? Don't wurry! Internet Mail comes with a built-in spell checker that pops up whenever you send a message and alerts you of any errors.

5 Click on the Send button on the toolbar. Note that you're not sending the message yet, only putting it in the Outbox, to be sent when you're online.

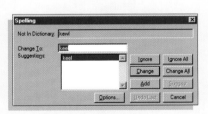

6 As soon as you choose Send, the spell checker starts complaining. (Don't take it personally. It's not that you can't spell; the spell checker is just a program that looks for unfamiliar words, and any foreign name or technical term can set it off.) Choose Add for words you know are spelled correctly, and choose Change when the program suggests suitable replacements for your errors.

How to Send an Attachment

E-mail, like its low-tech cousin (fondly referred to as "snail mail"), is not just for brief postcards. You can also use it to send packages—of the digital kind, of course. Examples of such packages—also known as *attachments*—are pictures, documents, and even entire programs (within the legal limitations, of course). The problem is, the Internet can't transfer those packages in their native format. You need to package them in a way that makes sense to the Internet, just the way you'd use a Federal Express envelope to mail something via FedEx. That "packaging" is called encoding, and there are two common types of encoding: uuencoding and MIME. Generally speaking, you don't care which one your e-mail program uses, but if your recipients tell you that they prefer one over the other, you need to know which one to use. Don't worry, it sounds like a mouthful, but it's easier than you think. Let's send a picture of my children (taken with a digital camera) to my mother-in-law.

TIP SHEET

▶ **A better way to handle multiple attachments (especially large ones) is to compress them. You'll need to use a program such as WinZip to do this (see Chapter 13 for more information).**

▶ **When your attachments are large, send an earlier message to warn your recipient that there's heavy load ahead, so he or she will be prepared to have the phone line busy for a while.**

▶ **Want your recipients to visit a certain Web page? Send its shortcut from your Favorites folder as an attachment, so they can go there directly by double-clicking on the attached shortcut. For your information, shortcuts have the extension .lnk.**

 ▶ **①** Create a new message, as described on the previous page. Click on the Paper Clip toolbar button to display the Insert Attachment dialog box.

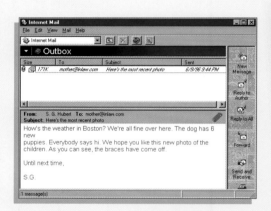

⑤ With snail mail, either the sender or the receiver pays for the package. With e-mail, in contrast, both parties pay connect charges while they're online to either upload or download a file. If you don't want to irritate your mother-in-law with a huge attachment that will take a long time to download, be frugal with your attachments. To see how much your attachments add up to, in bytes, click on the down arrow next to the Inbox icon, choose Outbox, and view the contents of the message that's waiting to be delivered. Luckily, if the message is here, it's not too late to fix it, so double-click on it and remove any attachments that take up too much space.

2 In the Insert Attachment dialog box, search for the file you want to send. You may need to open a different folder to find it. Once you find it, click on the Attach button to add it to your message. You'll get an icon for that file in the attachment pane, below the message pane.

3 Have more than one file to send? No problem. Repeat the process for each file. To send a message that contains attachments, just click on the Send toolbar button, as with a regular message.

4 To set the default encoding to something your recipients can use, open the Message menu, choose Options, and then click on the Send tab. Next click on the Advanced button, and make your selection in the Message Format area of the Advanced Settings dialog box.

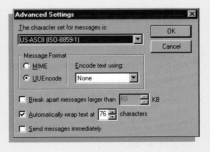

How to Manage Incoming E-Mail Messages

When you've been on the Internet for a while, you'll find out that many people know who you are and what your address is. This works pretty much like a pyramid plan: You tell three people your address, they tell three people each, and pretty soon, the whole world knows about you. The inevitable result is, your Inbox gets flooded with mail, and a lot of it is plain old-fashioned junk mail—unsolicited stuff that does nothing but take up your free time. So you need to learn to scan your Inbox quickly to identify the offenders, and read the important messages first. Luckily, there's a preview pane, so you can look at the first few lines in a message and decide whether it's worth your time. Here's how you handle incoming mail.

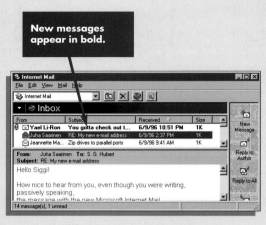

New messages appear in bold.

1 When a new message comes in, it shows up in boldface in the Inbox.

8 Are you so impressed with the message that you want to share it with others? Just click on the Forward icon , and type the name(s) of the people with whom you want to share this (separate them with semicolons). They'll get the entire message, including the attachment and any additional comments by you, and the message line will read *Fw:*, which stands for Forward, natch.

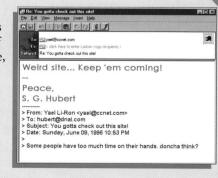

7 The original message appears at the bottom of the new message, with the > symbol before each line. In Internet lingo, this symbol means that you're quoting a message back to the person who sent it. The sender's e-mail address is automatically inserted in the To box, so you just need to type your reply and click on the Send button.

TIP SHEET

▶ Notice the different font sizes and colors in step 7? That configuration is customizable too. Set it in the Options dialog box (see "How to Customize Internet Mail" earlier in this chapter for instructions). It's a very handy visual tool when you're trying to tell who wrote what.

▶ To avoid an unnecessary delay, tell Internet Mail that you don't want it to check the spelling in the original message, only in your reply. To do that, choose Options from the Mail menu, click on the Spelling tab, and check the option to ignore the original text in a reply.

▶ Do you value your friendship with everybody you correspond with? Use the Forward button judiciously. Sending dozens of people unsolicited messages of little value is considered bad form on the Internet. The term for it is "spamming" and you don't want to be guilty of that!

This message has an attachment.

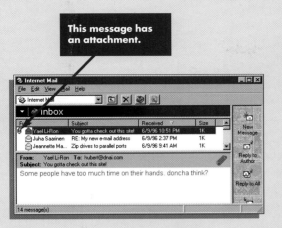

2 Click on the new message, and its contents appear in the preview pane. You may need to scroll down to view more, if you don't see the entire message.

3 If there's an attachment (you can tell by the paper clip icon next to the message in the Inbox), double-click on the message to open it in a separate window, where you can see the attachment as an icon in the attachment pane at the bottom.

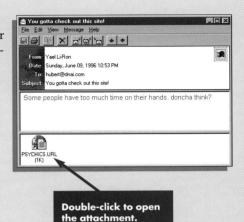

Double-click to open the attachment.

4 There are two ways to handle attachments: You can either open them or you can save them to disk for future use. To open (or launch) an attachment, double-click on it. You'll get a warning that the file may be infected with a virus. If you trust the person who sent it to you, click on Open to confirm that it's okay. If the attached file has the extension .url, it's a link to a Web site, so you'll go to that site when you double-click on it.

5 If you'd rather save the file to disk so you can return to it later, right-click on the attachment icon, choose Save As, and find the appropriate folder on your hard disk for that file.

6 To reply to the message, click on the Reply button on the toolbar. If you're not viewing the message in a separate window, you can click on the Reply to Author or Reply to All icons on the icon bar.

How to Manage Stored Messages

Are you a pack rat? Even if you think you're not, Internet Mail turns you into one. All the messages you've sent and received, even those you've deleted, get saved on your hard disk, taking up space unnecessarily. Sure you may want to hold on to that marriage proposal you got from your Brazilian pen-pal, but there are lots of worthless pieces of mail that you should get rid of, and soon.

Internet Mail uses different folders to sort your mail, and each of them needs your attention. Here are some tips for working with those folders effectively.

▶ **1** You already know about the Inbox. That's where all your incoming mail goes. When you're done reading and replying to a message, you need to make a decision: Save or delete? If you want to save it, you need a folder. To create a folder, choose File, Folder, Create. Type a name for the folder and choose OK. I have two folders: Work stuff and Personal stuff, but you can create any filing system that works for you.

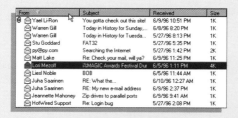

6 Want to view messages in a particular order? By date, name, or subject? Just click on the column heading by which you want to sort, and the whole list will get sorted in a split second. Click one more time, and the sort order changes from ascending to descending (*Z* to *A* instead of *A* to *Z*).

2 Don't want to save the message? Select it and press the Delete key on the keyboard. The deleted message doesn't vanish, however. It gets moved to the Deleted Items folder. You can get there by clicking on the down arrow to the left of the Inbox icon, and selecting Deleted Items.

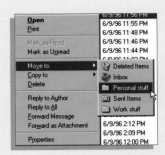

3 As you can see, the Deleted Items folder is just a trash can. Everything you've thrown into it is still there, taking up space on your hard disk. You need to empty the trash can to reclaim that space. To do so, press Ctrl+A to select all the messages, and then press the Delete key on your keyboard. You'll be asked to confirm this action, so click on Yes. A word of caution: Look over the messages to make sure, one last time, that you're not getting rid of an important message.

5 And what about all those messages you've sent? You think they're out of your hair? They're not. They're still there, in the Sent Items folder. You may want to save some of those messages into other folders, but you'll need to delete the rest. Go to the Sent Items folder and do your house cleaning, saving and deleting messages as described in the previous steps.

4 Go back to the Inbox folder by clicking on the down arrow to the left of Deleted Items and choosing Inbox. See a message you want to save? Right-click on it, choose Move To, and select the appropriate folder.

How to Use the Address Book

When you first start your e-mail career, you'll probably have a few people you want to correspond with. It's relatively easy to memorize two or three e-mail addresses, cryptic as they may be, but as you gain experience and new pen pals, you'll need to keep track of all those people and their addresses. That's where Internet Mail's Address Book comes in handy. In addition to storing names and e-mail addresses, the Address Book lets you maintain important information, such as mailing address, phone number, and random notes. You can even create groups, such as Friends or Clients, for easy mass-mailings. Here's how.

 To launch the Address Book, choose File, Address Book, or click on the Address Book icon on the icon bar (if you don't have one, reread "How to Customize Internet Mail" earlier in this chapter).

TIP SHEET

▶ Instead of typing the recipients' addresses in the To box, just click on the tiny rolodex card icon next to the box and pick a name from your address book.

▶ You can also type a partial address (such as the first 2–3 letters). When you click on Send, Internet mail will look for a match in your address book. If there are several matches (everybody knows five Bobs), Internet mail will show a list of the possible candidates and let you pick one.

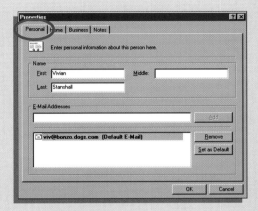

2 To add a new contact, click on the New Contact icon on the Address Book's icon bar.

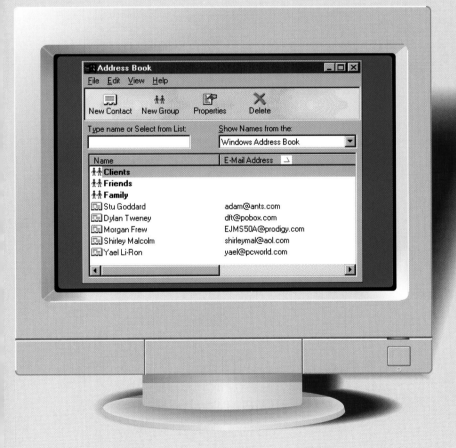

3 Type the person's name and e-mail address, and click on the Add button.

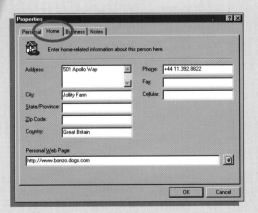

4 Click on the Home tab and enter any information you have. Repeat this for the Business tab. Next click on the Notes tab and type any notes about this person. This area is ideal for client information (*prefers not to be harassed at home after 11pm*, and so on).

CHAPTER 10

How to Use the Newsreader

Extra! Extra! Read and write all about it!

As discussed in Chapter 1, newsgroups have very little to do with the news; they are gathering places for people who share the same interests and enjoy exchanging views and information via electronic bulletin boards. Any program you use to read and write newsgroup messages is called a *newsreader*. Internet Explorer includes a newsreader called Internet News that is so similar to the Internet Mail program discussed in Chapter 9 you'll immediately feel at home with it.

Newsgroups have their own weird language and etiquette (commonly referred to as "netiquette"). Here are my top seven rules of netiquette:

- **Thou shalt not spam.** And now in English: Don't flood newsgroups with repetitive messages, and don't send junk e-mail. Spamming is the Original Sin of on-line exchange.
- **Thou shalt not flame in vain.** Meaning, don't reply to others' messages with nasty comments, unless they really really deserve it. Expect to be flamed whenever you spam a newsgroup.
- **Thou shalt get the FAQs.** Frequently Asked Questions, or FAQs, are available in every self-respecting newsgroup. Don't spam the newsgroup by asking a question before you check the FAQ first.
- **Thou shalt not praise beef to vegetarians.** You know, mind your manners. Don't join a newsgroup just to provoke its members. Antagonists often find themselves banned.
- **Thou shalt talk only when thou hast something to say.** It's very common to see 20 people reply to a question or comment with a "me too!"—which serves no purpose other than to spam the message board.
- **Thou shalt not bear false identity.** It's OK to have an anonymous "handle," but don't pretend to be somebody else, thereby getting that person in trouble.
- **Honor thy newsgroup.** Some newsgroups have their own set of netiquette rules that are different from the standard. Make sure you know what they are. You'll normally find these posted as regular articles.

How to Configure Internet News

Before you can drive a new car, you need to figure out what all the buttons do, then adjust the seats and mirrors, and program the radio for your favorite stations. So let's get familiar with the Internet News program, and, while we're at it, customize it so we can feel at home. Look at the figure in the center of the page for a road map to Internet News. To launch the program, double-click on My Computer, and then on the Internet News icon.

 1 Select News, Options to go to the Options dialog box, where you'll specify some of your preferences.

TIP SHEET

► **The most important thing to configure about Internet News is the news server and your user ID (your account name). You can modify other options later, when you're more familiar with the program and know what you like and dislike.**

► **The toolbar, icon bar, and menus offer many of the same features. To gain more screen "real estate," you can hide the toolbar and/or icon bar by selecting the View menu and clicking on each of them to "turn them off" (remove the check mark). To display them again, just repeat the process (this reinstates the check mark).**

► **You can also disable the Header Information bar at the top of the preview pane to gain more space. To do so, click on View, Preview Pane, and then click on Header Information to turn it off (remove the check mark).**

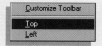

8 Don't like the icon bar's location? Right-click on any empty space in it (not on an icon!), and select Top or Left.

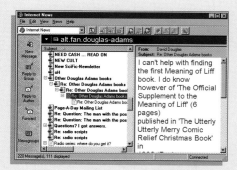

7 If you'd rather have the preview pane side-by-side with (rather than below) the message pane, select View, Preview Pane, and then click on Split Vertically.

② Click on the Server tab to tell the program where your news server is located. This information should be given to you by your Internet service provider, so make sure you have it before you start. For example, my provider, DNAI, has informed me that my news server is news.dnai. com. First fill in the blanks for your name, e-mail address, and organization (that last one is optional).

③ Now click on the Add button and type the name of your news server, and then click on OK.

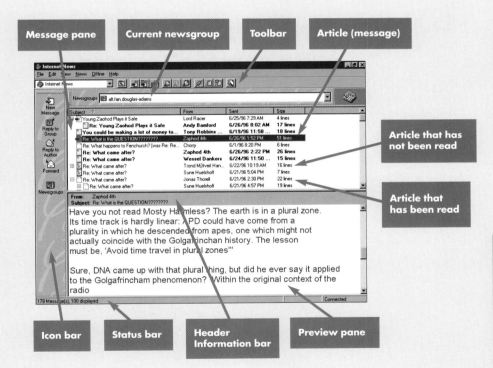

④ When you're asked whether you want to subscribe to newsgroups, click on the No button. You'll learn how to subscribe on the next page.

⑤ Click on the Fonts tab, and then, one by one, click on the three Change buttons to modify the size and color of fonts to be displayed on your screen. These selections are only for your convenience, and won't affect the text your recipients see. Note that "messages which have no formatting" refers to messages you view in the preview pane.

⑥ Let's compose a "signature"—text that appears at the bottom of each message you post onto the newsgroup. It can include a clever quote from your favorite author, a shameless self-promoting slogan, or just your name, whatever you like. Click on the Signature tab, and then click inside the check box next to Text. Type your signature into the box, and then click on the OK button to exit this dialog box.

How to Subscribe to a Newsgroup

There are thousands and thousands of newsgroups in the universe. The actual number changes daily, as new groups form and others disband. How do you know which ones are there? Log on to your news server, and browse, ever so slowly. The initial process may be a bit time-consuming, but once you've established which newsgroups you want to join (or *subscribe to*, in newsgroup lingo), the process gets simpler. Whenever you log on to that server, you'll be notified of new groups, and that list will be short and sweet if you log on often. For your first time, don't be afraid to subscribe to as many newsgroups as you like, because there's quite a bit of trial and error in the process, and you don't know how good—or bad—a newsgroup can be until you check it out. This is not a long-term commitment. You can drop out (or *unsubscribe*) whenever you want.

Ready? Let's gate-crash some parties. (Don't worry; they want you to.)

TIP SHEET

▶ Rather than browse at random or type keywords that may or may not yield results, use a search engine such as AltaVista (see Chapter 7 for more information) to search for words within newsgroup articles.

▶ To sort messages by date, size, subject, or author, click on the appropriate column heading. Click once for ascending order (*a* to *z*), and twice for descending order (*z* to *a*).

▶ Tired of waiting for the same articles to download every time you check out a newsgroup? Configure the program to show only unread messages by selecting View, Unread Messages Only.

▶ **1** Click on the Newsgroups icon or press Ctrl+W.

7 A plus sign next to an article indicates that it's the beginning of a *thread*, or discussion—that is, there are replies to that message. If you click on the plus icon, the thread "expands" to reveal the replies. A minus sign means that there are no more replies (in other words, you're at the end of the thread).

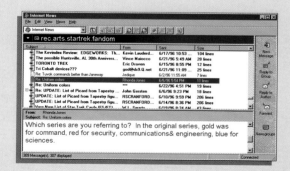

6 You can start reading messages (called *articles* in newsgroup jargon) by clicking on messages in the message pane to read their contents in the preview pane.

2 So many newsgroups, so little time. If time is not an object, browse through the list at a leisurely pace, using the vertical scroll bar to scroll up and down. When you see a group you'd like to check out, double-click on its icon to subscribe. The newspaper icon next to the newsgroup name indicates that you've subscribed.

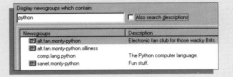

3 Better yet, if you have a general idea what you're looking for, type a keyword in the Display Newsgroups which Contain box. The list will shrink to show only those newsgroups whose names contain what you typed. I'm a huge Monty Python fan, so I typed **python** and got a list with four matches. One seemed to be about an unrelated subject, so I subscribed to the other three.

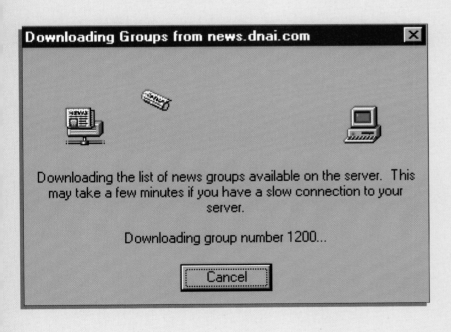

4 So how many newsgroups have we subscribed to already? Click on the Subscribed tab at the bottom of the screen to get that list.

5 Want to go to one of the newsgroups on the list? Just click on its name, and then on the Go To button at the bottom of the screen, and watch the display get updated with messages. Don't try to read anything as long as the status bar indicates that it's still downloading messages.

How to Post an Article

A newsgroup article is usually a question you're posing to your peers or an announcement you wish to share with them. Whether you're trying to get information or promote an issue, there's no better place than among people who share your passion (obsession?) for a topic. You'll be amazed how fast you get a response, and how often it'll be full of great information. People on the Net just love to share.

I've discovered the newsgroup alt.books.kurt-vonnegut, and I'm going to try my luck there.

TIP SHEET

▶ **Make your postings as succinct as possible. People have very short attention spans and get bored after five or six lines (blame MTV if you want).**

▶ **Make the subject line as clear as possible. Using just plain "Vonnegut" as a subject in this newsgroup would be like wearing black at night: You just won't get noticed.**

▶ **Message mysteriously disappears from list? You must be configured to hide messages that have been read. To overcome that, select View, and then click on All Messages.**

▶ **Some newsgroups are "moderated," which means that all postings are first screened before the moderator deems them appropriate. In short, expect a slight delay before your messages show up on moderated groups. The higher level of discussion in most moderated newsgroups should more than make up for this delay.**

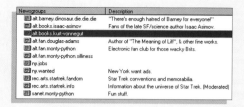

▶ **1** Having subscribed to that newsgroup (see the previous topic), click on the Newsgroups icon, click on the Subscribed tab, click on that newsgroup, and then click on the Go To button.

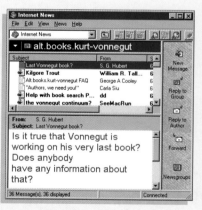

9 Lo and behold, a few minutes later, the message shows up!

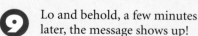

 8 Next you'll get a confirmation that the message has been posted. Click on the OK button.

2 In a few minutes, you'll get a list of all the available articles/ messages in that newsgroup. Remember, it's important to look for the FAQ first, before asking a question that's been answered hundreds of times before. The FAQ is just another article, usually titled FAQ or something similar. Double-click on it to open it in full view.

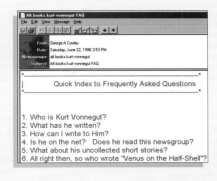

3 Once you've established that the question hasn't been asked yet, close the FAQ file by pressing Alt+F4 or clicking on the Close button on the title bar, and return to the newsgroup's message area. Now click on the New Message icon in the icon bar.

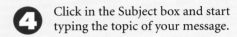

4 Click in the Subject box and start typing the topic of your message.

5 Click in the message area and start typing. Notice your "signature" at the bottom? That's the one you configured earlier in this chapter, under "How to Configure Internet News." If you want, you can change or erase it now.

6 To post the message, click on the Post Message button on the toolbar.

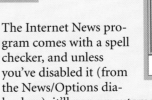

7 The Internet News program comes with a spell checker, and unless you've disabled it (from the News/Options dialog box), it'll pop up automatically and highlight any word that it doesn't recognize. In a case such as Vonnegut, you can either tell it to Ignore (that is, skip) the unknown word or Add it to the dictionary. For typos and spelling errors, consult the spell checker for suggestions, and select Replace when you find the correctly spelled word on its list.

How to Respond to an Article

If you like to show off your knowledge, you can't beat newsgroups. Here you can respond to questions from less-informed people and overwhelm them with your expertise, maybe even make friends for life. More often than not, though, you get to be one of thirty people who respond with the same information. If that doesn't keep your ego at bay, I don't know what will. Let's see how it's done.

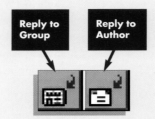

▶ **1** See a message you wish to reply to? Double-click on it, and then click on the Reply to Group or Reply to Author button on the toolbar. The Reply to Group button posts the reply for everyone to see (possibly subjecting you to flames, accusing you of spamming the newsgroup with information everybody knows). The Reply to Author button launches Internet Mail, the e-mail program discussed in Chapter 9. Let's go with the e-mail option (OK, so I'm a chicken).

TIP SHEET

▶ Although it's good to quote back a message to its author so he or she knows what you're replying to, this approach can result in stuffed-up newsgroups, with all the huge, repetitive messages. In your reply, erase any lines from the original message that shouldn't be repeated, and keep only those that can serve as a reminder about which message you're talking about.

▶ If you do want to reply to the group rather than to the author, first check whether someone has already replied with the same information you wish to share.

▶ Never, ever, add your two cents' worth to a discussion with just "ditto" or "me too" or "hear, hear" unless you're ready to be called names you've never seen in print before.

Notice that the original message
has been inserted at the bottom,
with the customary > characters
in front of each line, signifying
that you're quoting the recipient's
message to him or her. Type your
response above it.

Click on the Send
button on the toolbar.

The spell checker pops up, so
check your message for typos.

Open Internet Mail and click on the
Send and Receive icon in the icon bar
to send the message. See Chapter 9 for
more information on this.

How to Unsubscribe

Joining a newsgroup is a lot like love at first site. You like what you see and you want to spend the rest of your life with that group. OK, at least the rest of the year. But as often happens in matters of the heart, you may wake up two days later wondering whatever attracted you to that obnoxious/boring/silly/braindead (pick the one that applies) newsgroup. Fortunately, you haven't exchanged valuable jewelry with those people, and divorcing them is as simple as clicking on a button.

Granted, I think that Barney, the purple "dinosaur" of PBS notoriety, is pure evil, so I subscribed to alt.barney.dinosaur.die.die.die. It took me a total of ten minutes to discover that I didn't want to participate in any of the discussions. I'm just too busy. Besides, I'm pretty determined to have a life. So I need to unsubscribe.

▶ ❶ From the main Internet News screen, click on the Newsgroups icon in the icon bar.

❻ The orphaned line remains on your list of newsgroups you subscribe to until you exit the program or, if you can't wait, until you click on the Reset List button.

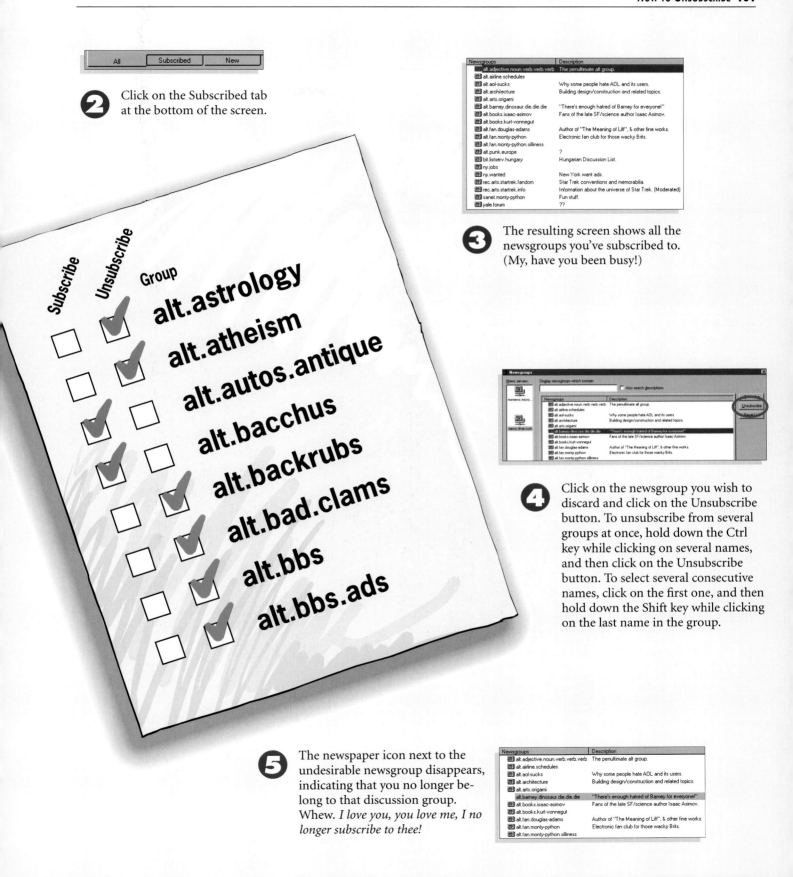

2 Click on the Subscribed tab at the bottom of the screen.

3 The resulting screen shows all the newsgroups you've subscribed to. (My, have you been busy!)

4 Click on the newsgroup you wish to discard and click on the Unsubscribe button. To unsubscribe from several groups at once, hold down the Ctrl key while clicking on several names, and then click on the Unsubscribe button. To select several consecutive names, click on the first one, and then hold down the Shift key while clicking on the last name in the group.

5 The newspaper icon next to the undesirable newsgroup disappears, indicating that you no longer belong to that discussion group. Whew. *I love you, you love me, I no longer subscribe to thee!*

CHAPTER 11

Downloading and Using Files

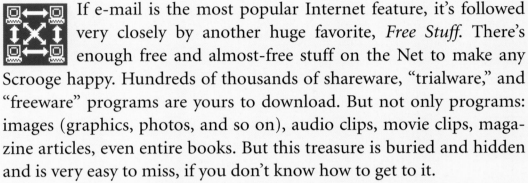 If e-mail is the most popular Internet feature, it's followed very closely by another huge favorite, *Free Stuff.* There's enough free and almost-free stuff on the Net to make any Scrooge happy. Hundreds of thousands of shareware, "trialware," and "freeware" programs are yours to download. But not only programs: images (graphics, photos, and so on), audio clips, movie clips, magazine articles, even entire books. But this treasure is buried and hidden and is very easy to miss, if you don't know how to get to it.

In this chapter we'll play Aladdin, saying *Open, Sesame!* to the treasures that the Web has to offer, then grabbing the tools that let us haul out (or *download*) all the goodies.

How to Create and Manage a Download Folder

Before you can start your treasure hunt, you need a temporary storage area for all the stuff you find. Ideally, you should have a Downloads folder on your hard disk, into which you'll save your files. The reason is simple: Most download-able files need to be "unzipped" or extracted in order to run. After you install a program, there's often some cleanup ahead, such as getting rid of all the temporary files created by the setup pro-gram, and a temporary location makes this cleanup easier. (You wouldn't want to delete all the files in just any folder, indiscriminately.)

1 Let's start by creating a folder on the Desktop, into which we'll later save our downloaded files. Right-click anywhere on the Desktop (but not on any icon) and select New, Folder.

8 Click on OK to close the dialog box, and you're done. We'll use this folder in the next few pages. Close Internet Explorer if it's open, and then launch it again from its new shortcut.

7 Now right-click on the new short-cut on your Desktop, select Properties, and click on the Shortcut tab. In the Start In box, type **c:\windows\ desktop\ junk'n~1**. If you named your "junk" folder any-thing else, replace the *junk'n~1* with the first 6 characters of that name, without spaces, followed by "~1". For ex-ample, if you called that folder *Open Sesame*, you would type **c:\windows\desktop\opense~1**.

2 While the words New Folder are still highlighted, type **Junk 'n stuff** (or whatever you'd like to call that folder).

3 Now place the folder icon anywhere on the Desktop that works for you. (As you can tell, I use pretty consistent naming conventions.)

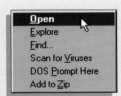

4 Next we want to make sure that Internet Explorer always takes you to this folder when you try to download a file. To do that, you need to create a *shortcut* to Internet Explorer. To make it easy on us, there's a shortcut on the Start menu, so we'll copy it to the Desktop. Right-click on the Start button and select Open.

6 Click the right mouse button on the Internet Explorer icon and hold it down while you're dragging the icon to the Desktop. When you let go of the button, you'll get this menu, so select Copy Here. When you're done, close the Programs folder.

5 Double-click on the Programs icon. Your Programs folder probably doesn't look like mine, but it should have the Internet Explorer icon.

How to Use ftp to Download

Most of the time, when you select a file to download, you get a simple dialog box that asks you where you want to save the file. But some sites still use the ancient (and quite cryptic) method called *ftp* (file transfer protocol). Don't be intimidated by it, because Internet Explorer hides ftp's ugly face from you. You do need to know a few things about this UNIX relic, though. To demonstrate this, we'll go to the Winzip ftp site to download Winzip—one of the most popular shareware programs on earth.

▶ **1** An ftp site doesn't have an http address, but, well, an ftp one. To go to Winzip, type **ftp://ftp.winzip.com** or just **ftp.winzip.com**

5 Lo and behold, you're at your "Junk 'n stuff" folder. (If you're not, it may just mean that you're not configured right, but you can still navigate your way to that folder.) Click on Save to copy the file to your hard disk. A few moments later and you're done. You've achieved ftp!

2 An ftp site is just a directory, with some files and perhaps some subdirectories. It looks just like your hard disk, but this one's using UNIX instead of Windows. See the central graphic for the less-than-spectacular view.

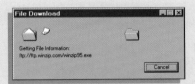

3 Since we're using Windows 95, we want to download Winzip95.exe. This is a self-extracting file, so after we download it, it'll decompress and lots of other files will materialize from it. Click on that filename to select it for download. Internet Explorer will examine the file briefly, displaying this dialog box.

4 Next you need to decide whether you want to open (that is, run) the file right now or save it first, then run it yourself. I strongly recommend the latter method, because you have more control over the outcome of the installation, and are less susceptible to viruses.

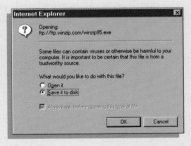

How to Use Winzip to Unzip Files

As we said before, Winzip is an indispensable utility for anybody who downloads programs from the Internet. Here we'll see how to use it to unzip files—but Winzip should already be installed on your system. If it isn't, read the previous page for information on downloading and installing it.

1 For the purpose of this exercise, let's assume that you've already downloaded a zipped file (that is, a file with the .ZIP extension) and saved it to your Junk 'n stuff folder. In my case, I'll unzip the file Cleese.zip, which contains several memorable sound clips from Monty Python.

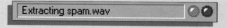

6 The files are being "decompressed," or unzipped into the specified directory. While Winzip does this, the green light on the status bar changes to red. When it's done, the light becomes green again. You can now close Winzip by clicking on the "X" button on the title bar.

TIP SHEET

▸ Once you've unzipped it, you can delete the zipped file from your hard disk.

▸ When you get e-mail attachments that are zipped files, just double-click on the Zip icon in your Internet Mail program (see Chapter 9) to launch Winzip.

2 To launch Winzip, just double-click on a zipped file's icon.

3 The screen you see at the center of the page pops up, revealing the contents of the zipped file.

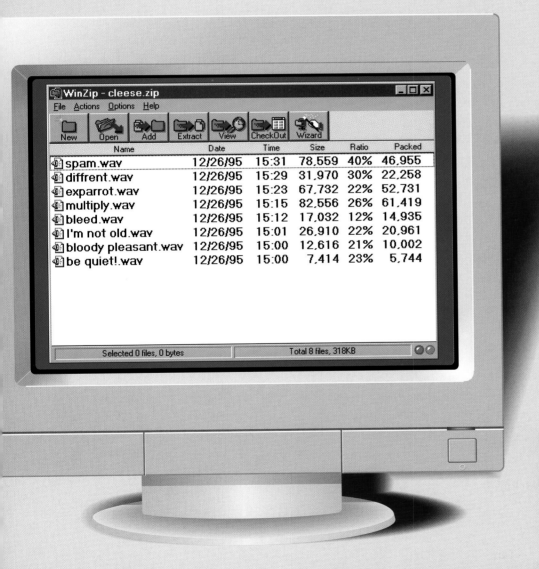

4 Click on the Extract button on the toolbar.

5 The next dialog box asks you where you want to extract these file to. Use the tree structure to navigate your hard disk until you find a spot for these files, then click on the Extract button.

How to Grab Graphics from a Web Page

Graphics are among the easiest things you can download, because you can just click on an image you see and save it to your hard disk without going through the additional hassle of a protracted download via a Web or ftp site. Just remember one thing: The fact that images are easily downloadable doesn't mean that you're allowed to get them. Copyright laws apply on the Internet just like everywhere else. So if you see a Homer Simpson graphic that you want to use on your home page, resist that temptation unless you can afford a lawsuit. You can use copyrighted images on your local system, for your personal amusement, but putting them in the public's eye is as smart as swimming with sharks.

 1 The central screen is a collection of free background images you can use on your Web page (see Chapter 17 for information on creating Web pages). That URL is **http://www.primenet .com/~robhood/textures.html**. See one you like? Right-click on it and select Save Picture As.

TIP SHEET

▶ **When you set a background or image as your wallpaper, Windows names that image Internet Explorer Wallpaper.bmp and saves it in the Windows folder. Be sure to rename it to something more descriptive, because next time you set an image as your wallpaper, you'll replace this one.**

▶ **Most images on the Web are in either .GIF or .JPG format. If you want to edit these, you'll need a graphics program such as PaintShop Pro, which you can download from www.jasc.com.**

 6 If the wallpaper is "tiled," or repeated all over the screen, right-click anywhere on your Desktop and select Center.

2 If you created a download folder as described at the beginning of the chapter, point to it, or select any appropriate folder for this image.

3 Your boring Desktop can come to life with graphics you see on the Web. See an interesting background on a Web page? Right-click on it (make sure you're not clicking on any other item on the page) and select Set as Wallpaper.

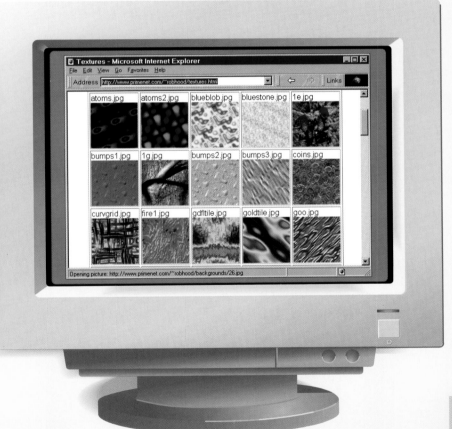

4 Your Desktop now has an interesting texture for its "wallpaper."

5 Another way to dress up your desktop is to set an image other than a Web page background as the wallpaper. Right-click on an image, select Save as Wallpaper, and that image will turn your Desktop into Something Completely Different.

TRY IT!

Web surfing has its charms, but the real online gold mine is software you can download for nothing more than the cost of your Internet connection. In this Try It, you'll be downloading, unzipping, and registering a shareware product called Paint Shop Pro, a full-featured graphics tool from Jasc.

Click in Internet Explorer's Address box, type **www.zdnet.com**, and press Enter. Then click on the ZDNet button marked Software Library.

Scroll down the ZDNet Software Library page until you see the Search section. In the keyword box, type **Paint Shop Pro**, then click on the Start Search button.

Near the top of the list of matching files, you'll see Paint Shop Pro 32-bit v.3.12b2. Click on this link to continue.

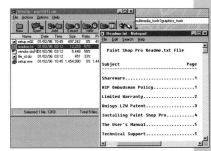

Click on the Download button to begin the download. You'll then get some feedback as the download proceeds.

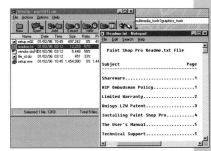

When Internet Explorer is done downloading, WinZip automatically launches and shows all of the Paint Shop Pro files in the WinZip archive. Double-click on the readme.txt file to open it. Read it thoroughly for instructions and the latest information.

Close the readme file and return to the WinZip window. Select all the files by typing Ctrl+/, then click on the Extract button.

In the Folders/ Drives box, scroll down to the Temp folder on drive C. Click on it to select it, then click on the New Folder button.

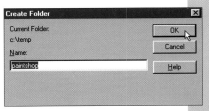

Type **paintshop** in the Name box of the Create Folder dialog box and click on OK.

Continue to next page ▶

TRY IT!

Continue
below

12

Accept the
default desti-
nation direc-
tory of PSP
by clicking
on the OK
button. You'll
then see
many of the familiar graphical events that
mark a software installation.

9

Highlight the
paintshop
folder, then
click the
Extract button.

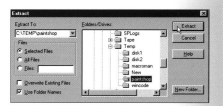

13

When asked
if you want
to add Paint
Shop Pro to the Program Manager,
click on the Yes button.

10

Press the
Start button
and click on
Run.

14

Accept the default Program Manager
Group of Paint Shop Pro by clicking
on the OK button in the dialog box
that opens next.

11

Find the path
to the setup
executable
file for Paint
Shop Pro by browsing, or type
C:\TEMP\paintshop\Setup.exe. Then
click on the OK button to begin setup.

15

When Paint
Shop Pro is
fully in-
stalled, click on the Yes button to
launch it.

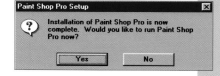

Paint Shop Pro is shareware, not freeware— you must register and pay for it if you decide to keep using it after a 30-day free evaluation period. Click on the Help button to discover more information about registering your copy of Paint Shop Pro.

A Help file opens listing vendors from around the world who sell Jasc products, including Paint Shop Pro. If you're located in the USA, click on the Jasc, Inc. link.

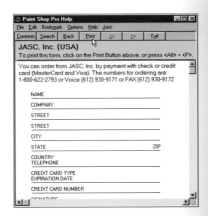

Print the form and fax it with your credit card number to Jasc; you can do this now, or at the end of the 30-day trial period.

CHAPTER 12

Extending Internet Explorer's Functionality with Plug-Ins, ActiveX Controls, Java, and Helper Apps

 Up until now, you've used Internet Explorer for browsing static Web sites. And while these sites can be graphically rich and chock-full of information, few have been truly interactive, and few, I'll wager, have grabbed your interest or offered unique, compelling content. Well, all that's about to change.

In this chapter you'll discover some of Internet Explorer's more advanced features, including support for plug-ins, players, ActiveX Controls, Java, and Virtual Reality Modeling Language (VRML). Plugins and players are small programs that extend Internet Explorer's functionality, sort of like extra options with your new car. (Plug-ins work as *integrated* applets within the environment of the browser; players work separately as "helper" applets outside the environment of the browser.) VRML is a graphics rendering scheme that delivers 3-D images, and ActiveX Controls and Java both add features and functionality to Internet Explorer. All of these technologies extend the core capabilities of Internet Explorer to include support for audio, video, multimedia, and 3-D content, as well as interactive experiences such as stock tickers, news bulletins, and more.

Each lesson walks you through the basics of one of these technologies. By the end of the chapter, you'll be using Internet Explorer to investigate corners of the Web you didn't know existed.

How to Download the Shockwave Plug-In

If you've ever enjoyed a multimedia-rich CD-ROM title, there's a good chance it was developed with a tool from Macromedia. And Macromedia's Shockwave delivers the rich graphics and audio of a CD-ROM title over the Internet to your browser. All you need is a copy of the Macromedia Shockwave plug-in.

Plug-ins, small add-on applications, were originally developed for Netscape Navigator, but Microsoft Internet Explorer supports them as well. In this lesson you'll download the Shockwave plug-in. In the next lesson, you'll install, configure, and use it.

1 Launch Internet Explorer and type **www.macromedia .com/shockwave/download/** in the Address box and press Enter. Scroll down to the Get Shockwave section. Enter your first and last name, your e-mail address, and which platform you're using, and then click on the Get Shockwave button.

7 After the file has been expanded, choose Run from the Start menu, type **c:\program files\microsoft internet\plugins\setupex.exe** in the Open box, and click on OK.

2 You'll see a list of servers from which to download Shockwave. Click on one to select it.

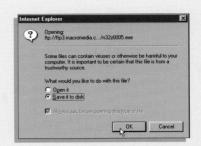

3 Internet Explorer begins transferring the Shockwave file to your PC. Click on OK when asked whether to save the file to disk.

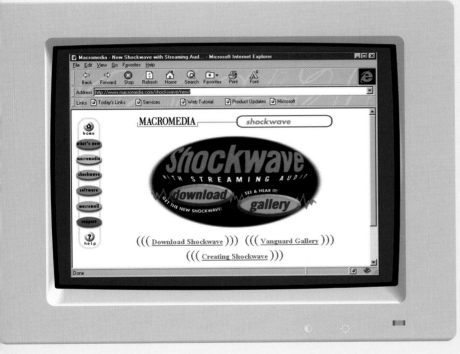

4 In the Save As dialog box, choose the directory C:\Program Files\Microsoft Internet\Plugins. You need to keep the Shockwave plug-in in the preconfigured Plugins folder.

6 Because the Shockwave file is a self-extracting executable, you'll see a DOS window as the file is expanded into your Plugins directory.

5 After the file has been transferred, choose Run from the Start menu, type **c:\program files\microsoft internet\plugins\n32z0005.exe** in the Open box, and click on OK.

How to Use the Shockwave Plug-In

Once you've downloaded Shockwave, you can install it, configure it, and begin to put it to use. Shockwave lets you enjoy rich graphics and audio of CD-ROM quality right from within Internet Explorer. For an example of a great "Shocked" site (a site that uses the Shockwave technology), check out www .pccomputing.com.

▶ ❶ The install routine InstallShield asks if you want to install Shockwave. Click on Yes.

TIP SHEET

▶ **The Read Me files are optional. If you want to look at them before enjoying Shockwave, accept the default in step 6, and Shockwave will automatically open several Read Me files, outlining Shockwave's various capabilities.**

▶ **Be certain you install Shockwave in the Plugin directory (C:\Program Files\Microsoft Internet\Plugins). Internet Explorer can only work with plug-ins if it knows where to find them, and this is where it assumes they will be.**

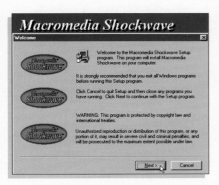

2 Welcome to the Macromedia Shockwave installation routine. Click on Next, read the licensing agreement carefully, and then click on Yes.

3 Click on the Internet Explorer radio button and then click on Next.

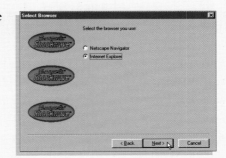

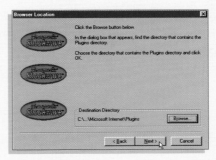

4 Click on the Browse button and select your destination directory: C:\Program Files\Microsoft Internet\Plugins. Then click on Next.

5 Shockwave should start installing onto your hard drive. You'll see a progress indicator indicating what percentage of the program has installed.

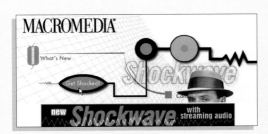

7 Now that Shockwave is installed, close and relaunch Internet Explorer and type **www.macromedia.com** in the Address box. You'll notice the difference right away, as the Macromedia home page comes alive with clever animation and streaming audio. Streaming means you listen to audio like you would on the radio; the sound continually "streams" to your browser. The same with graphics—they're sort of like TV.

6 Once setup is complete, uncheck the radio button Yes, Open the Read Me Files and then click on Finish. (You can always read the Read Me files later if you want to.)

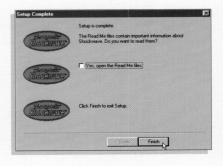

How to Download the RealAudio Player

If your system has a sound card and speakers, you'll definitely want to enjoy audio on the Web. But most Web-based audio is made up of downloadable sound clips that you have to download, save on your system, and then play. Fortunately, that's not the case with Progressive Networks RealAudio Player. Instead of waiting to download and play a sound file, RealAudio brings sound to Internet Explorer instantly, allowing you to enjoy broadcasts from ABC and NPR, baseball games, rock concerts, and more.

In this two-part lesson, you'll download, install, configure, and use the RealAudio Player.

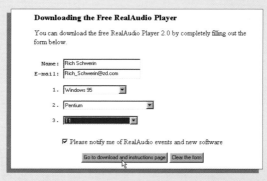

 Type **www.realaudio.com/products/player2.0.html#download** into the Address box and press Enter. Then scroll down until you see "Downloading the Free RealAudio Player." Enter your name, e-mail address, platform, processor, and connection speed. Click on the button Go to Download and Instructions Page.

TIP SHEET

▶ **Before you can download the free RealAudio player, you must input your name, e-mail address, platform, processor, and connection speed. In this case, the information is not optional. A radio button (checked by default) gives you the option of being notified of RealAudio events and new software; you'll probably want leave it checked.**

▶ **As with Shockwave, it's critical to the RealAudio Player in the correct folder; it should be in C:\Program Files\Microsoft Internet\Plugins.**

2 Click on the download site closest to you.

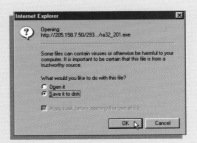

3 As the file begins to transfer, you'll be asked what you want to do with it. Make sure you're saving it to disk, and click on OK.

4 Like the Shockwave plug-in you learned about earlier, the RealAudio player should go in your Plugins folder. In the Save As dialog box, be sure the path is C:\Program Files\Microsoft Internet\Plugins, and then click on Save.

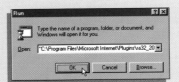

6 Welcome to the RealAudio Player Setup. Read the licensing agreement carefully, and click on the Accept button. Then continue this lesson on the next page.

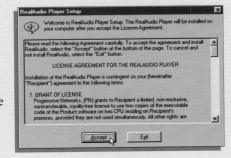

5 You'll see a dialog box indicating that the RealAudio player is being transferred to your desktop. Once the transfer is completed, choose Run from the Start menu, type **c:\program files\microsoft internet\plugins\ra32_201.exe** in the Open box, and then click on OK.

How to Install and Use the RealAudio Player

Now you'll continue to install and configure the RealAudio Player, and listen to a audio welcome message from Progressive Networks. With the RealAudio Player, as mentioned , you can listen to streaming audio broadcasts from NPR, ABC, and other broadcast networks. You can also tune in the radio programming from c|net and ZDNet, which you saved to your Favorites folder in an earlier Try It.

▶ **1** Enter your name and company name and click on Continue.

TIP SHEET

▶ **When you first begin the RealAudio Player setup, you're prompted for your name and company. While you are required to enter your name, your company name is optional.**

▶ **In the third step you'll be prompted for your Internet connection speed. It's critical that you select the right speed for the best audio quality. If you're unsure of your Internet connection speed, choose 28.8Kbps, and then contact your service provider to verify what the speed really is.**

▶ **Most of you will want to choose the Express Setup in step 4. But if you're more experienced you can choose Custom Setup and spend a little more time modifying default settings.**

2 Verify what you just entered and click on OK if it seems fine. Or, if you notice an error, click on the Change button, which returns you to the first step.

3 From the pull-down menu, select the speed at which you're connected to the Internet and click on OK. This example shows a screamingly fast T1 connection. Your connection speed will most likely be 14.4Kbps or 28.8Kbps.

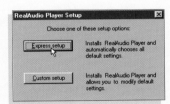

4 Click on the Express Setup button. Then click on Yes in the next dialog box.

5 Now that the RealAudio Player has been successfully installed, click on OK, and get ready to listen.

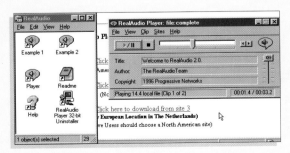

6 Notice the RealAudio Player interface while you listen to a welcome message from the Progressive Networks RealAudio Team. Volume adjustment is on the far right side of the RealAudio Player box.

How to Use the Microsoft Stock Ticker ActiveX Controls

Microsoft's ActiveX is another technology that enhances your Explorer experience by letting you add animation, audio, video, and virtual reality to otherwise plain vanilla sites. And because Internet Explorer supports ActiveX, you don't have to download any plug-ins or players. Instead, you use Internet Explorer to browse the Web just as you normally would, and when you encounter a Web site that uses ActiveX, you'll automatically download ActiveX Controls—little pieces of software actually embedded in the Web page.

1 Type **www.microsoft.com/ie/ie3/activex.htm** into Address box and press Enter. Then scroll down until you see the link "find out what ActiveX Controls" and click on it.

7 The Stock Ticker you'll see stream across your browser is a result of ActiveX technology. This is just a sample of the many amazing things that you can enjoy with ActiveX.

2 You're now experiencing an ActiveX Control. Watch as the Welcome message scrolls through the star-studded window. You can read about this live object on this page.

Caution, Live Objects on Web Pages!
ActiveX™ Controls activate Web pages! See the scrolling Internet Explorer logo we added to this page with the ActiveX Marquee Control? Notice that you didn't have to download a program in order to view it. That's because ActiveX Controls are software components that run right in Internet Explorer. They're small, slick, and versatile—the possibilities for creating cool content with ActiveX Controls are limitless. Any content you dream up can be created with an ActiveX Control because the control can

3 Scroll down until you see the link "ActiveX Controls Gallery" and click on it.

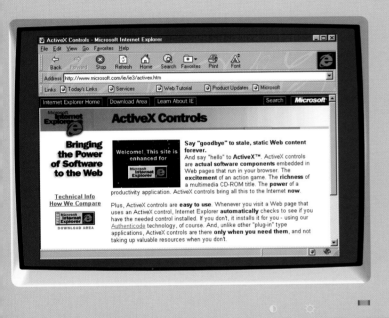

List of ActiveX components

Welcome to the ActiveX Component Gallery

You will be amazed at this collection of ActiveX™ controls and samples--a gallery of components and resources offered by our partners for your Web authoring and development tasks. This gallery will continue to grow as we add more controls, samples, and information. We hope that you will visit this area frequently for the most up-to-date listing of ActiveX components available.

When you enter the gallery, you will notice that you can navigate the components either by category or by company name, using the frame on your left. Each component has an information page and a sample page. Clicking the link for the sample page will automatically install the control on your system so that you can view the sample. (In future versions of the gallery, each control will have a bitmap that will allow you to decide which controls to install.) Note that the hard-drive space required by the samples can vary significantly.

4 Welcome to the ActiveX Component Gallery. Notice that this page is designed using frames and that the lower-left lower frame contains a scrollable list of ActiveX components.

Real Time Data Acquisition
• Stock Ticker

5 Scroll down through the list of ActiveX components until you see the "Stock Ticker" link under Real Time Data Acquisition. Click on it.

6 The Stock Ticker page appears in the right-hand frame. Click on the "Control Sample Page" link.

Stock Ticker

Real Time Data Acquisition
Microsoft Corp.

This control is used to display changing data continuously. The control downloads the URL specified at regular intervals and displays that data. The data can be in a text or XRT format.

Control Sample Page

For more information on this control contact:

Microsoft Corp.
http://www.microsoft.com

How to Use Java Applets

Like ActiveX Controls, Java applets are small software programs that you can transfer to your desktop through Internet Explorer. You've probably heard the buzz about Java; after all, it has one of the more compelling names in computing today.

Java applets can do many of the same things that ActiveX apps can do: audio, video, multimedia, animation, 3-D graphics, and so on. With Java, as with ActiveX, you don't need to download a separate program to enjoy Java applets with Internet Explorer.

So what does that mean for you? It means that you can **do things** with Java and Internet Explorer that **nobody else can**. And it means **faster**, more **stable**, and more **functional** Java support while you surf the Web. In fact, Pendragon Software's Java Performance Test shows that Internet Explorer beats Netscape Navigator in nearly every category tested. But don't just take our word for it. Download Microsoft Internet Explorer today and see for yourself.

Download Internet Explorer and the updated Java Support for Internet Explorer Now.

Then watch how Microsoft Internet Explorer delivers Java like no other browser.

▶ **1** Type **www.microsoft.com/ie/ie3/java.htm** in the Address box and press Enter. Scroll down until you see the link "delivers Java like no other browser" and then click on it.

TIP SHEET

▶ **Java is similar to ActiveX, so which one should you use? Actually, you can use *both* with Internet Explorer, so the question is which technology will be more prevalent on the Web. Stay tuned.**

▶ **Still curious about Java, how it works, and how it compares and contrasts with ActiveX and other Internet technologies? For more information, check out the Java-Soft site at www.javasoft.com. JavaSoft is a division of Sun Microsystems, the company that developed Java.**

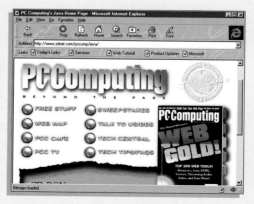

8 Another great Java-based site is www.zdnet.com/pccomp/java/. To go there, type this URL in the Address box and press Enter.

It's Happening Now
Now that you've installed Microsoft Internet Explorer 3.0, you can view the many Java™ applets available on the Web. In fact, you're looking at one right now! The colored graphical design you're seeing (called a Mandelbrot) is the result of mathematical calculations done in Java - sort of like a digital lava lamp!

② Notice the Mandelbrot graphical design pulsating on in your Internet Explorer window. This Mandelbrot graphic is actually a Java applet and is just one example of the things Java can do.

Other Java Resources

Check out some popular Java Web sites with more examples of Java applets and additional information (first, please read our disclaimer):

- Dimension X
- Gamelan
- The Java Centre
- JARS (Java Applet Rating Service)
- The Java Developer
- The Java User Resource Network
- Pendragon Software

③ Scroll down until you see a list of other Java resources. Click on the Dimension X link.

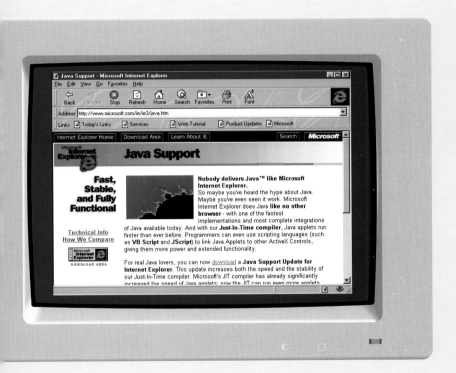

④ Dimension X is a development of Java and VRML (3-D) technology (which you'll learn about on the next page). Scroll down through their home page and you'll see Java-based animation. Then click on the Dimension X logo.

Out beyond the hype and froth of today's Internet mania, Dimension X is developing, building and employing the very latest in Internet related technology. Since opening our doors in the Spring of 1995 we have been committed to breathing life into the static click-and-load world of today's World Wide Web. Whether it be Liquid Reality™ (our 3D VRML toolkit) or our latest release, the drag-and-drop Java™ Animator we call Liquid Motion™, we strive to blend the best in technology with the hottest in Entertainment to deliver compelling content to your computer.

The Studio

⑤ This page contains more information about Dimension X, as well as a gallery of sites that use Dimension X Java technology. Scroll down and click on the link "The Studio."

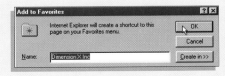

⑦ Accept the default name of this site (Dimension X Inc) by clicking on OK in the Add to Favorites dialog box.

⑥ Save this page of links for future reference. Click on the Favorites icon, and choose Add to Favorites.

How to Use VRML

Remember 3-D movies? In the 1950s, Americans flocked to movie houses where they watched villains and other strange creatures "jump" off the screen and "into" the theater. At least, that's the way it appeared when they slipped on those funny 3-D glasses. With Internet Explorer, you can enjoy even *better* 3-D content, and you don't need funky glasses.

Internet Explorer supports a technology called VRML—Virtual Reality Markup Language. As with ActiveX and Java, you don't need to download an extra program to enjoy 3-D VRML worlds. In this lesson you'll learn more about VRML, and you'll fly through a 3-D graphic of the Microsoft campus in Redmond, Washington.

TIP SHEET

▶ The tilt and spin commands can have a dizzying effect. Remember, the faster you drag with your mouse, the faster the image tilts or spins (depending on which tool you've selected).

▶ If you've experimented with the walk, tilt, spin, and slide tools, and are disoriented, remember that you can simply click on either the Reset or Straighten button to return to your starting location. You can also click on the Menu button and choose Viewpoints, Starting Viewpoints.

▶ For more information about VRML, check out the following URLs: cedar.cic.net/~rtilmann/ mm/vrml.htm, www.virtpark .com/theme/proteinman, and www.sdsc.edu/vrml.

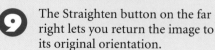

1 Type **www.microsoft.com/ie/ie3/vrml.htm** into the Address box and press Enter. Then click on the link "explore some 3-D virtual worlds."

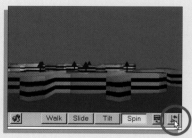

9 The Straighten button on the far right lets you return the image to its original orientation.

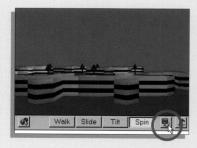

8 You can also return to your starting location and orientation by clicking on the Reset button, the second button from the right.

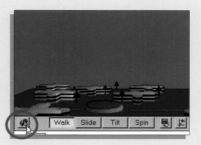

2 Scroll down until you see a 3-D graphical image of the Microsoft corporate campus. Notice the seven control buttons at the bottom of the graphic. Click on the Walk button.

3 While the Walk tool is selected, click on the 3-D graphic and hold down the mouse button while dragging forward. You seem to "fly" into the center of the campus. Then click on the menu button in the lower-left corner of the VRML controls panel.

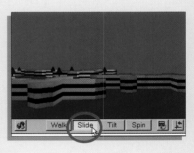

4 From the menu, choose Viewpoints, and then click on Starting Viewpoint. This returns you to your starting viewpoint.

5 Now click on the Slide button. Then click on the 3-D image, hold down the mouse button, and drag to the left or right to "slide" the image left or right.

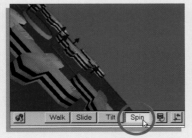

7 Click on the Spin button, click in the 3-D image window, hold down the mouse button, and, drag to one side or the other and watch the image spin around on an axis.

6 Now click on the Tilt button, click within the image, and drag to tilt the image.

CHAPTER 13

The Internet for Children

 Reactions to the Internet tend to fall into two camps: It's seen either as the greatest reference library and playground and community in the world, or as a seething den of iniquity that can corrupt anyone under the age of 21 in a single online session. In reality, the Internet falls somewhere between these two extremes. To enable your kids to take advantage of the good stuff without being exposed to the seamy side, Internet Explorer features some special security options based on an Internet rating system established by the Recreational Software Advisory Council (RSAC).

The Council's RSACi rating system is a voluntary classification scheme that requires responsible adult-oriented Web sites to embed some special HTML code in their pages. This code, called PICS (Platform for Internet Content Selection) indicates—to any browser that can read it—the level of language, nudity, sex, and violence at site.

This chapter explains how you can turn on Internet Explorer's security system to filter out the stuff you don't want your kids to see. You also learn about sites that contain kid-friendly information and about even more cool kid's stuff online.

How to Set Acceptable Ratings

If you're concerned that your children (or your sensitive older relatives) might be able to find strong material online, you'll probably want to turn on Internet Explorer's Content Advisor right away. The default setting the Content Advisor uses is RSACi level 0—absolutely nothing beyond the pale in the areas of language, nudity, sex, and violence gets through. You don't need to know much about the rating system to set up this basic level of security. All you need is a password you won't forget and less than five minutes to set things up.

▶ **1** To begin implementing a rating scheme, choose View, Options.

 Want to block out sexual and violent content, but don't mind your kid having exposure to robust language online? Using the RSACi rating system, you can. Just pick a category from the Content Advisor's window and slide the Rating marker to the right. You get instant feedback about the level of content you will be allowing through.

2 In the Options dialog box, click on the Security tab and then click on the Enable Ratings button.

3 *You're* supposed to be in control here … not your wily teenager (who can find the Ratings button faster than you can). So you get to set your password to make any changes to ratings. Enter a password in the dialog box, reenter it to verify the spelling, and click on OK.

4 You'll see the Content Advisor dialog box. But to set up the "maximum security" ratings that RSACi provides for, just click on the OK button. (You'll learn more about some of the other options here that in the next few pages.)

6 You'll see that your password is already active. Enter it here and you'll get access to the controls you want to wield. Press Enter or click on OK when you're done.

5 You'll be notified that Content Advisor is installed. This means that any RSACi ratings at a site will prevent Internet Explorer from opening the page. If this seems a little harsh, the information on this confirmation box tells you what you need to do: To make any changes to the security settings, click on the Ratings section's Settings button.

Understanding RSACi Ratings

RSACi rates five levels of leniency in four sensitive categories–language, nudity, sex, and violence. As you set acceptable levels using the RSACi system in Internet Explorer, you see a description of what you're prepared to see online. Here's an overview of the categories and ratings.

Violence Rating: level 1, harmless conflict, some damage to objects; level 2, creatures injured or killed, damage to objects, or fighting; level 3, humans injured or with small amount of blood; level 4, humans injured or killed; level 5, wanton and gratuitous violence, torture, or rape.

Nudity Rating: level 1, no nudity or revealing attire; level 2, revealing attire; level 3, partial nudity; level 4, nonsexual frontal nudity; level 5, provocative frontal nudity.

Sex Rating: level 1, romance, no sex; level 2, passionate kissing; level 3, clothed sexual touching; level 4, nonexplicit sexual activity; level 5, explicit sexual activity or sex crimes.

Language Rating: level 1, inoffensive slang, no profanity; level 2, mild expletives; level 3, expletives and nonsexual anatomical references; level 4, strong, vulgar language, obscene gestures, and/or racial epithets; level 5, crude or explicit sexual references or extreme hate speech.

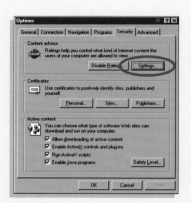

▶**1** To learn more about RSACi rating, read an overview in Internet Explorer's Content Advisor dialog box. Choose View, Options and click on the Security tab in the Options dialog box. In the Ratings section at the top of the dialog box, click on the Settings button.

TIP SHEET

▶ For an overview of the RSACi ratings in one simple table, enter http://www.rsac.org/images/ pamenu.map?515,15 in the Address box. Then scroll down to the ratings table.

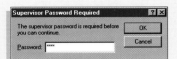

2 If you've already set up ratings, you'll have to enter your password in the dialog box and click on OK.

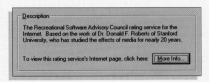

3 Click on RSACi in the Category section, and read the description of the system at the bottom of the dialog box.

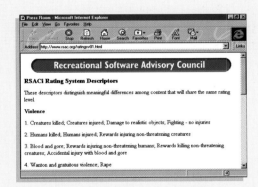

4 For a more thorough overview, click on the More Info button. This connects you to RSAC's Web site (http://www.rsac.org/) and takes you to the most current version of the ratings. Here, you can read through the four ratings categories (language, nudity, sex, and violence) and check out what's permitted in each of the four rating levels.

5 Now you can switch back to the Content Advisor by pressing Alt+Tab and adjust the level of your rating by clicking on a rating category and dragging the Rating slider to the right to be more permissive or to the left to be more restrictive.

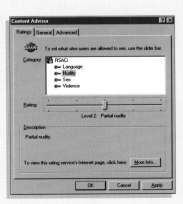

How to Use Rated Sites

O nce you've installed a rating system you think is right, it's time to check out the effect it has on your Web surfing. You can take two approaches: hit-or-miss, or cut straight to the chase. To cut straight to the chase, go to Microsoft's test site so you can check the effects. To take the hit-or-miss approach, you have to know a few adult-oriented sites that have adopted RSACi ratings. These tend to include the publishers of well-known adult magazines such as Playboy who want to uphold their reputation for protecting minors. For them, RSACi rating is the equivalent of putting their magazines on the top shelf of the newsstand, out of reach of the young.

▶ **1** Enter **http://www.microsoft.com/ie/most/howto/ratings.htm** in the Address box and press Enter.

TIP SHEET

▸ **If you want to supervise the sites that are being visited, it's a good idea to check the Internet Explorer history list periodically. Pull down the Go menu, and choose View History folder. This gives you a list of recently visited sites that you can revisit by double-clicking.**

▸ **Suspect that your password has been discovered? In Internet Explorer's View menu, choose Options, click on the Advanced tab, and then click on Properties. Enter your password and click on General. Click on the Change Password button and enter a new password.**

2 This takes you to the Internet Explorer Ratings page on Microsoft's Web site, which explains the process and philosophy of RSAC's ratings scheme at length.

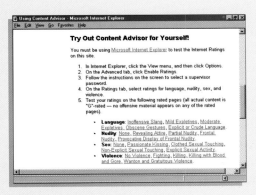

3 Scroll down until you reach the section about trying out Content Advisor. You'll see a series of hyperlinks labeled with RSACi rating levels for language, nudity, and so on.

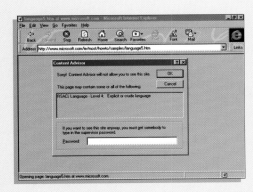

4 If you've turned on the basic level of security, you can click on any of these links from Inoffensive Slang to Wanton and Gratuitous Violence, and you'll see how the Content Advisor screens out the stuff you don't want to see. You'll get a grayed-out browser screen with a dialog box listing what's being screened out at the rated site.

5 To give the Content Advisor a real-world spin, try to open a site such as http://www.playboy.com. Here you'll get the same kind of results, this time with a list of the several reasons that you don't want your kid visiting the site.

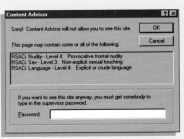

How to Use Unrated Sites

Even with the maximum levels of security set, you can get in to some horrendously kid-inappropriate sites. That's because not every site with sensitive material has adopted RSACi rating. RSACi is a voluntary rating system that requires sites to add a big chunk of code to their HTML pages. Not every Webmaster knows how to do this, or feels a responsibility do this. But don't panic: There's a way to block even sites that haven't been rated. This may also screen out perfectly innocuous and even educational sites, but there's a way to make them available using password protection.

▶ **1** In the Content Advisor dialog box (choose View, Options, Advanced tab, Properties), deselect the check box Users Can See Sites Which Have No Rating under User Options, and select the check box Supervisor Can Type a Password to Allow Users to View Restricted Content. Click on OK in each dialog box until you're out of the Content Advisor.

TIP SHEET

▶ **If you want a greater level of protection, read about software such as SurfWatch (http://www.surfwatch .com/) or NetNanny (http://www .netnanny.com/), which add filtering to external rating systems. These commercial programs block sites based on patterns of words that they find online, and maintain a database of suspect sites that they block.**

2 Try to view an unrated page now, and you won't get anywhere. Instead you'll see a dialog box like this. You have to use your supervisor password to unlock any page that isn't rated.

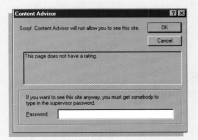

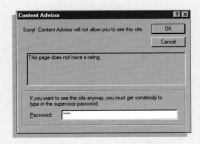

3 Because many useful, kid-safe, and wholesome sites haven't been rated yet (especially search sites that have no offensive content per se, but that might find some), complete restriction isn't ideal. However, you'll be able to gain access to the sites using your supervisor password. (Of course, this means you'll have to be "on call" whenever your kid's on the World Wide Web, but that's not a bad idea anyway.)

How to Use Yahooligans

E ven if you're concerned about restricting your kids' access to the Web, their experience with the world of cyberspace need not be a series of "thou shalt nots." There's a lot of good, honest, kid-friendly stuff out there. Your children can have some fun, learn something, and become exposed to a wider world than they would otherwise. With restrictions turned on, the random Web surf technique really doesn't work too well. So a focused series of searches can help. Because most Web searches aim to be inclusive, you could expose your kids to inappropriate material using them. Yahooligans, from the Web legend Yahoo, preselects only kid-friendly material.

1 Enter **http://www.yahooligans.com** in the Address box, and press Enter. At the Yahooligans home page, you'll be presented with a navigational graphic at the top of the page, a search form, and the top of a list of categories.

6 The Yahooligan's home page logo contains other navigation tips: To visit sites that have been added recently, click on New. Want an appealing site? Click on Cool. Clicking on the Random button takes you away from Yahooligans to some mystery site. The other buttons give you more information about Yahooligans, including the ability to add a new site you've found.

2 If you (or your kid) know what you're looking for, the fastest way to get results is to use the search form. Enter a word or two describing what you're looking for and click on the Search button.

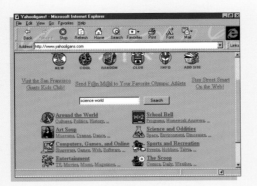

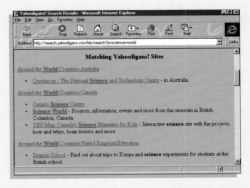

3 Yahooligans returns a list of matching words from its list of categories and site descriptions. the matching words appear in bold so they're easier to spot. To visit a site, click on the link (underlined blue text) next to the description that best matches what you're looking for.

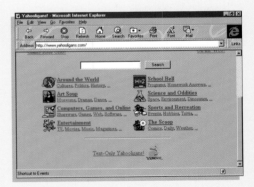

4 If you're not too sure what you're looking for, browse the category headings on Yahooligans' home page. (You may need to scroll down to view the bottom of the page.) Click on one that seems interesting. If you don't see something that quite matches what you're looking for under a category heading, click on the ellipses (…) at the end of each subcategory list for more headings.

5 As you go down into Yahooligans headings, you'll find underlined blue hyperlinks next to a description in regular black text. If a description appeals to you, click on the hyperlink next to it. Each page supplies a search form that lets you narrow your search within the category you're exploring.

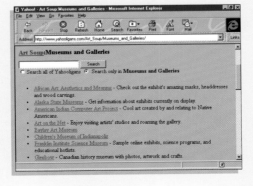

How to Find Other Recommended Sites (Uncle Bob's)

Another great place to find kid's stuff is Bob Allison's Uncle Bob's Kid's Page. This page covers all manner of sites that Allison has judged suitable for and interesting to children. Most parents who look over the site (including the authors of this book) agree with him.

▶ **1** Type **http://miso.wwa.com/~boba/kidsi.html** in the Address box and press Enter to get to the home page of Uncle Bob's Kid's Page.

TIP SHEET

▸ **CyberKids (http://www.woodwind .com/cyberkids/) is a general-interest magazine for kids, including music, art, and stories—complete with a serial novel and a feedback section called CyberKids Connection for writing responses.**

▸ **Kids' Gallery (http://plaza.interport .net/kids_space/gallery/gallery.html) is a site where your kids can look at other kids' art and upload their own art for possible inclusion in the gallery.**

2 Scroll down until you reach the Section Index, which gives you a brief indication of what's in each section. Because this site grew organically from Allison's discoveries, the organization tends to be a little haphazard, but it makes for great browsing.

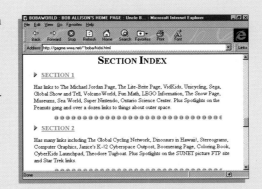

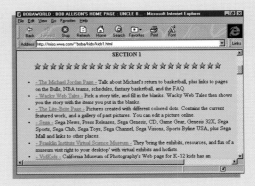

3 When you see something you're interested in, click on the section that houses it. This takes you to the section, which includes links and a longer evaluation and description of the site.

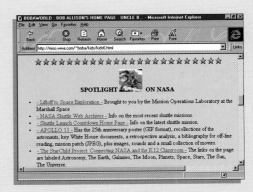

4 Pay particular attention to the spotlight sections—collections of Web site links with a theme in common.

5 When you find a suitable link, click on it to go to the site. If Internet Explorer is not set up to block sites that don't carry an RSACi or other rating, kids may be able to follow links from sites that Uncle Bob recommends to sites that he wouldn't recommend. The Web is too well-linked by nature to make any guarantees.

CHAPTER 14

Using Security Options

As the Internet and the World Wide Web have grown, so have dreams of electronic commerce and online shopping. Imagine buying anything and everything you could find at a large mall—and more—without ever having to leave your desk. Well, you can buy just about anything online, and when you're shopping, you'll want to protect yourself by taking advantage of the many security options built in to Internet Explorer.

In this chapter you'll explore Internet Explorer's various security settings, and then you'll access a few secure sites and do some online shopping at Virtual Vineyards. Privacy is closely associated with security, so you'll also learn more about online privacy issues, Pretty Good Privacy (PGP) encryption, and electronic mail remailer services. Plus you'll download a CyberCash Wallet sample from CyberCash.

Put one hand on your wallet and the other on your mouse and let's go shopping!

How to Use Security Settings

Here you'll explore a few of the security features that come with Internet Explorer. By default, many of these security features are turned on, and at first you probably won't want to change them. However, as you become more accustomed to using Internet Explorer, you'll want to know more about these features and how to change them.

First you'll take a closer look at Microsoft's Security site, and then you'll dig in to Internet Explorer's Security Options. In the next lesson, you'll continue to explore Internet Explorer's Security Options.

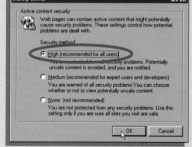

▶ ❶ After launching Internet Explorer, type **www.microsoft.com/ie/ie3/ security.htm** in the Address box and then press Enter. You'll see this Microsoft Internet Explorer Secure Communications site. Click on the link "learn how to use the security features."

❾ You can choose from three safety levels. By default, the Security method is set for high, but you can change it if you like. Click on OK, and continue the remainder of this lesson in the next section.

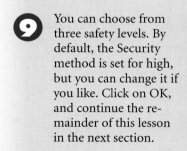

❽ Notice the Active content section of the Security tab. This is where you control which, if any, active content is delivered to Internet Explorer. To make the most of your Web surfing experience, make certain all the radio buttons are checked. Then click on the Safety Level button to open the Safety Level dialog box.

2 Choose Options from the View menu, click on the Security tab in the Options dialog box, then click on Enable Ratings.

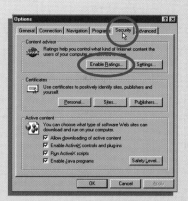

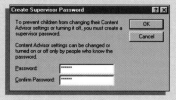

3 In the Create Supervisor Password dialog box, enter and confirm a password, and then click on OK. This allows you to set content controls and is useful if several members of your family (including your children) use Internet Explorer to access the Web.

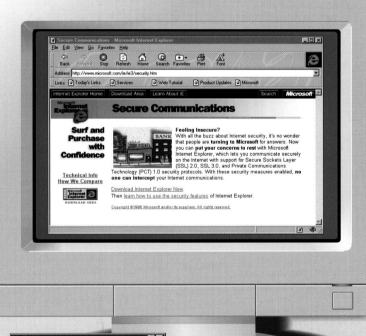

4 Back in the Options dialog box, under the Security tab, click on the Settings button. You'll get the Content Advisor dialog box, with a sliding scale for Language, Nudity, Sex, and Violence. See Chapter 13 for more information about RASCi ratings.

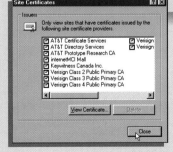

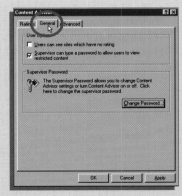

7 Back in the Options dialog box, under the Security tab, click on the Sites button to open the Site Certificates dialog box. Site certificates are an emerging technology; they assure you of a site's integrity. In the future, most commercial sites will offer some sort of certificate of authentication. Click on Close.

6 Click on the Advanced tab for further information about different rating systems for controlling content on the Web. Click on OK when you're finished.

5 Click on the General tab for more option settings to limit content access. You can also change your Supervisor password from here.

More about Security Settings

Here you'll learn more about Internet Explorer's security options, including Warnings and Cryptography settings.

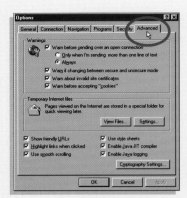

1 If you followed along in the last lesson, the Options dialog box should be open (if it's not, choose Options from the View menu). Click on the Advanced tab. By default, the six options under "Warnings" will all be selected, giving you ample warning of the events outlined in the Warnings section.

TIP SHEET

▶ **Warnings are nice when you're first starting, but after a while you'll find that they get in the way of your surfing experience. To change warnings, click on the Advanced tab in the Options window, and select or deselect from the six radio buttons marked Warnings.**

▶ **While you visit different Web sites, Internet Explorer saves copies of files from those sites locally on your hard drive. These files are saved in your Temporary Internet Files folder, which can grow quite large the more you use Internet Explorer. If you're running out of hard disk space, clear your Temporary Internet Files folder by selecting Settings, Empty Folder.**

▶ **Internet Explorer supports three cryptography protocols: SSL 2, SSL 3, and PCT. By default these are all allowed, and their radio buttons are checked. To enjoy the widest range of sites possible, accept these defaults by leaving the boxes checked and clicking on OK in the Cryptography Protocols dialog box.**

8 Click on OK to close the Options dialog box.

7 Internet Explorer warns you that you must restart for any and all changes to take effect.

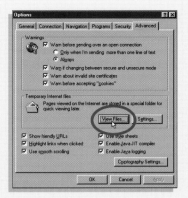

2 The Temporary Internet files section is where Internet Explorer stores text, graphics, and other Web elements of pages you've visited. Click on the View Files button.

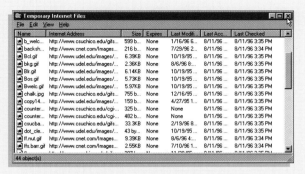

3 You'll see a (probably lengthy) list of files stored in your Temporary Internet Files directory. Click on the Close button when you're done.

4 In the Options dialog box, under the Advanced tab, click on the Settings button. From the Settings dialog box, you can control the amount of disk space dedicated to storing temporary files, empty or move the folder, and set how often Internet Explorer checks for updates of these pages. For now, leave the default settings unchanged and click on OK.

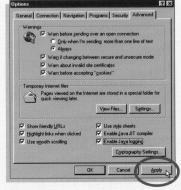

5 Under the Advanced tab in the Options dialog box, click on the Cryptography Settings button to open the Cryptography Protocols dialog box. By default, Internet Explorer supports all major two-key cryptography technologies. Click on OK.

6 Back in the Options dialog box, to Apply the changes you have made, click on the Apply button.

How to Access a Secure Site

So, what good are all these security settings? Well, when you access most unsecure sites, you won't notice a thing. But when you access secure sites, such as Travelocity, Internet Explorer's security capabilities become both more apparent and more important.

On this page you'll surf to Travelocity, a comprehensive Internet-based travel reservation service. At first, you'll see the regular Travelocity site, but then you'll access the Travelocity Secure Server.

TIP SHEET

▶ **You'll probably get tired of security warning boxes pretty quickly. The next time you see a Security Information window warning you of an unsecure connection—which is what you'll experience with a huge majority of Web sites—click on the radio button Do Not Show the Warning.**

▶ **How can you tell if you're connected to a secure site or not? If you see a gold lock icon in the lower-right corner of Internet Explorer's window, you're connected securely. If not, you're not.**

▶ **1** Type **www.travelocity.com** in the Address box and press Enter.

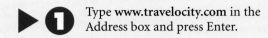

9 Now you'll see the detailed New Member form. Should you choose to become a Travelocity member, fill out each of the form windows, and then click on Submit.

8 You'll see the Login for Travelocity, further guaranteeing your security. If you're interested in becoming a member (it's free), click on the New Member link.

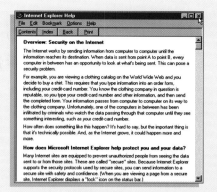

2 Internet Explorer alerts you that you're about to send "unsecure" information over the Internet. For more information about security, click on About Security.

3 Take a few moments to review some of the Internet security points outlined in the security help file, and then click on the Close button.

4 Constant security warnings can be annoying, and you'll want to avoid them in the future. Click on the radio button Do Not Show this Warning and then click on Yes.

5 Now you'll see the regular Travelocity site. (In case you're wondering, the URL changed because www .travelocity.com is an alias.) Since your browser supports SSL encryption, you'll want to reenter through Travelocity's secure server. Click on the link "secure server."

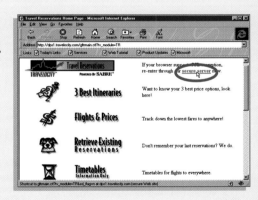

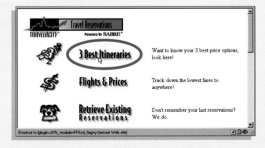

6 The site might look the same, but the small, gold lock icon in the lower-right of the Internet Explorer window indicates that you're now connected securely to a secure server.

7 While you're securely connected, you can make travel arrangements with your credit card without having to worry. Click on the "3 Best Itineraries" link.

How to Use a Remailer and PGP Encryption

Most Americans take their Constitutional right to privacy for granted. But the emergence of the Internet as an unparalleled global communications system has focused a great deal of attention on privacy issues.

This lesson introduces Pretty Good Privacy (PGP), an encryption technology developed by Phil Zimmerman to provide secure online communications.

Another interesting concept in privacy is anonymity. Here you'll also learn about e-mail remailer services, which let you send e-mail anonymously.

▶ **1** Type www.inforamp.net/~fire/anon.html in the Address box and press Enter.

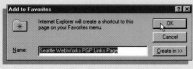

8 Accept the default name by clicking on OK. After you've done so, you can read more about PGP at your leisure.

7 Add the Seattle Web-Works' PGP site to your Favorites folder for future reference. (While on the site, click on the Favorites button and choose Add To Favorites.)

2 This brings you to one of many available anonymous e-mail sites, Anonymous@Email. Scroll down until you see the send mail box, where you'll send yourself a test anonymous e-mail. Type your e-mail address in the To: box, type **Anonymous E-mail** in the subject box, and then type yourself a little note in the large window. Finally, click on the Send Mail button.

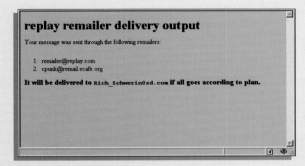

3 If your anonymous e-mail was delivered successfully, you'll see a replay remailer delivery output message like this one.

4 Now type **www.stack.urc.tue.nl/~galactus/remailers/** in the Address box and press Enter.

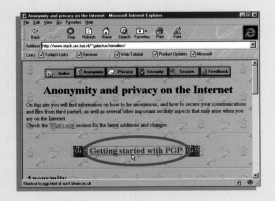

5 You'll see a Web site of comprehensive information about anonymity and privacy on the Internet. You'll also see the link "Getting started with PGP." Click on it.

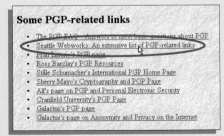

6 After you've read about PGP, scroll down until you see a list of PGP-related links. Click on Seattle Webworks; this is an extensive list of PGP-related sites.

How to Shop Securely at Virtual Vineyards

There's no end to the goods and services offered over the Internet, and in this lesson you'll use Internet Explorer's security features to do a little wine shopping. A few lessons back, you surfed the Travelocity site for travel reservations. In this lesson you'll surf the Virtual Vineyards site for wine and specialty foods.

▶ **1** Type **www.virtualvin.com** in the Address box and press Enter. Then click on the "Wine Shop" link.

TIP SHEET

▶ **Many (in fact most) secure sites require membership. This includes Travelocity and Virtual Vineyards, as you've seen so far. Most of these memberships are free, and aren't intended as a revenue method. Instead, memberships let the servers recognize and acknowledge you the next time you visit.**

▶ **Once you've become a member of more than a handful of sites, you might find it difficult to remember all your passwords and login names.** *Do not, however, write these down on a piece of paper,* **just as you wouldn't write down passwords for your ATM card in your purse or wallet. Some membership schemes remember your login and password information for you; consult with different sites for their different policies.**

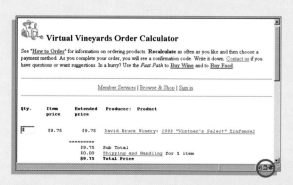

8 You'll see the Virtual Vineyards Order Calculator, where you can continue your wine purchase securely if you wish. Also, notice the gold lock icon in the lower-right corner of Internet Explorer's window, indicating that you have a secure connection to the Virtual Vineyards site.

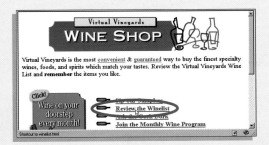

2 From the Virtual Vineyards' Wine Shop, click on the link "Review the Winelist."

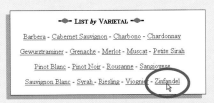

3 Do you like red wine? Scroll down until you see List by Varietal. Click on the link "Zinfandel."

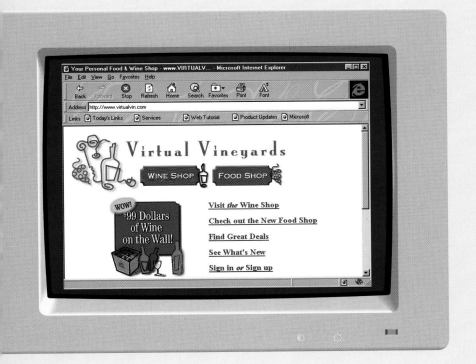

4 From the Zinfandel link, select a wine by clicking once in the check box next to that particular wine. In this example, I've selected David Bruce Winery's 1993 Vintner's Select Zinfandel.

5 After selecting a wine, scroll to the very bottom of the Wine list and click on the Remember Checked Items button.

6 Now scroll back up to the top of the list and click on the "Order Form" link.

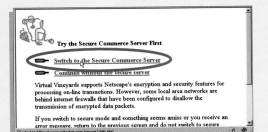

7 Up until now, you've been communicating with the Virtual Vineyards' Web server in an unsecure mode. Now click on the link "Switch to the Secure Commerce Server."

How to Use CyberCash

The numerous security technologies and measures built in to Internet Explorer go a long way toward furthering online transactions. After all, if you feel safe giving your credit card number to someone over the phone to purchase some goods or services, you should feel equally safe passing your credit card number over the Internet for similar goods and services.

One of the emerging technologies in this arena centers around the concept of electronic cash. Several companies have developed electronic cash products, including CyberCash. Here you'll learn more about the CyberCash technology, download your very own CyberCash Wallet, and visit a few online shops that accept CyberCash as a method of secure electronic payment.

1 Type www.cybercash.com in the Address box and press Enter. When you reach the CyberCash site, click on the FREE Wallet link.

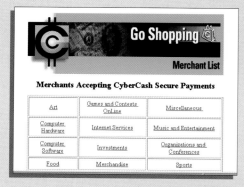

7 When the file has downloaded, click on the link "To see a list of CyberCash Merchants click here." Or type www.cybercash.com/cybercash/shopping/ in the Address box and press Enter. This brings up a list of various merchants who accept CyberCash as a method of payment. Now that you've downloaded your free CyberCash Wallet, you can install and configure it.

2 Now click on the link "Get the NEW! CyberCash Wallet."

3 You'll want the CyberCash Wallet for Windows. Click on the link "Wallet for Windows 827K."

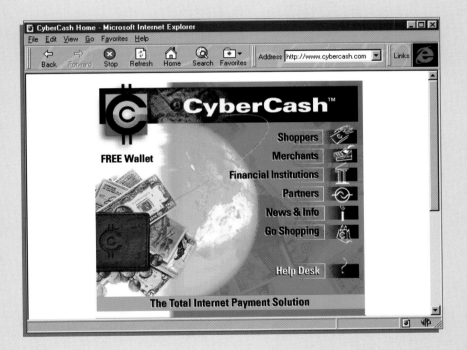

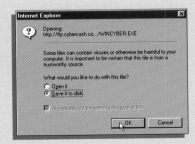

4 As you read about the CyberCash technology and the CyberCash Wallet, scroll down until you see the "Download Wallet" link and click on it.

6 Save it in the default directory by clicking on the Save button. You'll see the File Download window as the CyberCash Wallet is downloaded to your system.

5 As usual, when Internet Explorer begins to download this file, you're given an option to Save it to disk. Click on OK.

CHAPTER 15

Chatting with NetMeeting

If that huge phone bill is any indication, you've definitely "reached out and touched someone" quite a bit this month. Or maybe you have teenagers in the house, with the phone permanently attached to their heads. In either scenario, your telephone is obviously an important—and popular—part of your life. And as you become more experienced with Microsoft Internet Explorer, it will become an important part of your life as well.

So far, you've done a lot of surfing, downloading, searching, and saving. But now you're going to take your online activities to another, more personal level. In this chapter you'll download and learn to use Microsoft NetMeeting, an online chat and Internet phone/communications application.

Using NetMeeting you can chat with one or hundreds of people, around the corner or around the world, for just the cost of your Internet service connection. You'll also learn to send and receive files to and from others using NetMeeting. By chapter's end, you'll be fully versed in the finer points of TCP/IP–based communications and ready to move forward, learning to use the whiteboard in the next chapter.

How to Download and Configure NetMeeting

NetMeeting is yours free of charge, but you'll have to download it separately from Internet Explorer from the Microsoft Web site. In this lesson, you'll launch Microsoft Internet Explorer and proceed to the special Internet Explorer download area. Then you'll locate, download, and configure Microsoft NetMeeting.

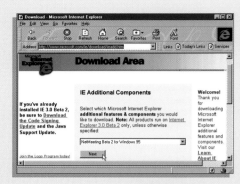

TIP SHEET

▶ If one of the download sites you select is busy or unavailable, or your connection seems unbearably slow, click on the Cancel button (during the download) and select another download site from the list. If things are still problematic, try downloading at a different time of day, when fewer users might be online.

▶ Before restarting your computer to finish installing NetMeeting, you'd be wise to save all other work and close all other files and applications. While Windows 95 should take care of this automatically, it's nice to have peace of mind, especially when working on mission-critical files.

1 As of this writing, NetMeeting is available free of charge, but it is a separate download from Internet Explorer. After you launch Internet Explorer, type **www.microsoft.com/ie/download/ieadd.htm** in the Address box. Here you'll find a selection of Internet Explorer's additional components. Click on the pull-down list and choose NetMeeting (in this case, it's NetMeeting Beta 2 for Windows 95). Then click on the button marked Next.

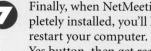

7 Finally, when NetMeeting is completely installed, you'll have to restart your computer. Click on the Yes button, then get ready to use NetMeeting in the next few pages.

2 Select the language you prefer (in this example, we've selected US English). Click on the Next button.

3 Next you'll have to choose from one of the many download sites. Click on the Net-Meeting download link (msnm10_b2.exe in this example; you may see something different) to begin downloading your copy of NetMeeting. You'll then follow the familiar download routine that you explored in depth back in Chapter 11. You'll also see a Windows Software Security alert. You'll be prompted several more times: Click on Yes or OK to continue through the routine.

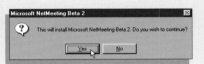

4 After the NetMeeting file has been transferred to your desktop, click on the Yes button to install it. Immediately after clicking Yes you'll see a detailed licensing agreement; click Yes again to continue.

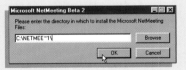

5 Accept the default directory for installing NetMeeting by clicking on the OK button.

6 As with any other installation program, NetMeeting provides feedback about the status of files being copied (in this case from a temp directory to the default directory you accepted in the last step).

How to Find Out Who's Online

Now that you've successfully downloaded and installed NetMeeting, you'll obviously want to learn how to use it. From the previous page, you should have just restarted your computer; notice the NetMeeting shortcut icon on your Windows 95 desktop. In this section you'll learn the basics of NetMeeting, including how to locate others to communicate with.

 1 Find the Microsoft NetMeeting icon on your desktop. Double-click on it to launch NetMeeting for the first time.

 5 Double-clicking on the Directory button brings up a list of everyone who's online and attached to the Microsoft User Location Server. From here, you can click on anyone's name and then on the Call button to initiate a conversation. You'll continue to explore this feature in the next lesson.

2 Before you can use NetMeeting, you'll need to fill out some information about yourself. At a minimum, you must supply your first and last name and your e-mail address. Here's an example with all the requested information filled in. Click in the First name box and type your name. Then use the Tab key to skip from box to box, filling in as much or as little information as you like. When you're finished, click on the Next button.

3 Next, NetMeeting asks your permission to include your name on a User Location Server. Since you'll want to communicate with others, click on the Yes radio button when prompted. You'll also see a User Location Server address. By default, this maps to uls.microsoft.com. Leave this as is and click on the Finish button.

4 Now the NetMeeting interface will be maximized on your desktop. In the toolbar, double-click on the Directory button at the far left end of the toolbar, so you can find someone to communicate with.

How to Join a Conversation

NetMeeting software? Check. Installed and configured? Check. Attached to a User Location Server? Check. Looks like you're all set to communicate. Where we left off on the previous page, you were scanning a list of other users with whom to communicate. On these two pages, you'll learn how to initiate a chat and carry on a discussion with someone around the corner or around the world.

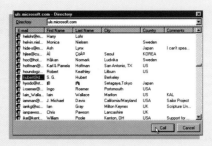

 1 Starting right from where you left off in the last step of the previous lesson, select a name from the Directory list. Then click on the Call button. (If you logged off and are starting from scratch, launch Microsoft NetMeeting by double-clicking on the NetMeeting icon (see step 1 in the previous exercise) and connect (by default) to the Microsoft User Location Server. Then select a name. Finally, click on the Call button. If that person doesn't accept your call, try someone else.

9 While you can always save in the default Windows folder, you might want to save chat transcripts in a separate folder. Click on the Create New Folder button, name the new folder Chats, and then click the Save button. By default, your transcripts will be saved with the .csv extension.

8 When you've finished chatting, you can save the transcript of your chat. Simply click once on File from the menu bar and select Save As.

TIP SHEET

▶ When looking for another chat friend in a User Location Server directory, click and drag the margin of the Comments column to read personal comments entered by others.

▶ After saving your chat transcripts in the .csv format, you can read them using any text editor, including WordPad, or any word processor, such as Corel WordPerfect or Microsoft Word.

Your message appears here when you press Enter.

Type your message here.

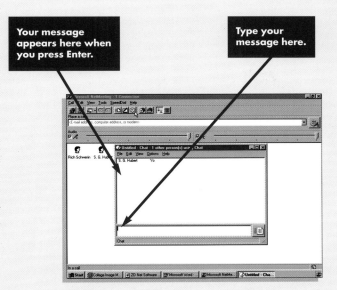

2 If and when the other person accepts your call, you'll then see two user icons in the NetMeeting interface. One of the icons will be you, the other will be the person with whom you're communicating. In this example, one of the authors has called the other. Communication is simple. Click in the bottom chat window and begin typing. Press Enter and your chat message is sent to the other person as it appears in the larger chat window.

3 By default, the chat window includes the participant's names and the message text in a standard, small font. To change the font, click on Options in the chat menu bar, and select Font.

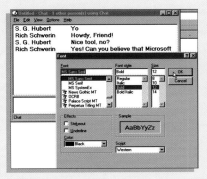

4 Select a more legible font style and size—try Bold, 12 point. Then click the OK button.

5 You can also change the chat format to display more than just the name of the person chat-

ting and their chat text. Click to open the Options menu and select Chat Format.

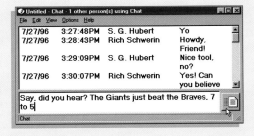

7 Notice that the chat window now shows the date and time, as well as the names of the chat participants and their text chat.

6 To add more information to the chat display, click on the Date and Time check boxes. By default, the message format is to wrap with the message next

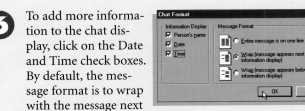

to the information display, but you can also change the format so messages appear below the information, or so that messages don't wrap. Take our advice, and accept the default setting of Wrap (with messages next to the information display). Then click on the OK button.

How to Exchange Files with Another Person

Once you've mastered the basics of chatting, you'll want to learn even more. Microsoft NetMeeting also lets you send files back and forth quickly and easily. On these two pages, you'll learn how to send a simple text file to a fellow chat friend. Then you'll learn how to work with a file you've received from another person. A word of warning: Only trade files with someone you trust, as this is a sneaky way for someone to pass along a computer virus and infect your Desktop.

 1 If you're still online and using NetMeeting from the previous pages, you can continue with the same chat partner, or select a new chat buddy for this exercise. If you're not online, you need to launch NetMeeting, connect to the default Microsoft User Location Service (ULS), and find someone to trade files with using the Call function (which you learned about earlier in this chapter). In this example, we've selected a new chat partner—Cory Williams.

TIP SHEET

▶ **Transferring files? The smaller the better. Even at faster speeds, really huge files take a long time and can be corrupted, or your connection can "hang," in which case you'll have to reboot. Take our advice: At slow connections (28.8Kbps and slower), don't attempt to transfer anything bigger than 1MB.**

▶ **If you receive a file from an unknown source, consider a few stopgap measures that can help protect your system from viruses. First, Microsoft has proposed a certificate technology called Authenticode. With Authenticode, files are certified as "safe" and authentic, giving you peace of mind when accepting files from a stranger. Second, get yourself a decent anti-virus tool from McAfee or Symantec and make a habit of checking all files for viruses.**

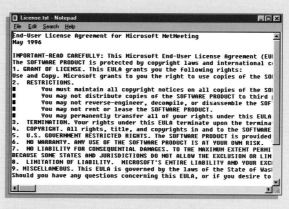

7 By default, Windows 95 opens up .txt files in Notepad, as shown in this example for the license.txt file. If someone sends you a file with an extension not supported by any of the applications on your system, you'll have to click on the Save or Delete button (in the dialog box shown in the previous step). When you're finished examining the file you've received, save it and close the application so you can return to the NetMeeting interface.

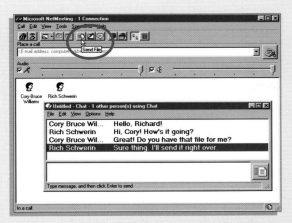

3 After you click the Send File button, the "Select a file to send" box appears. For this example, we've selected the License.txt file that comes with NetMeeting, but you can just as easily send any file from your Desktop or network—simply click on the Look In box and select any available resource from the drop-down menu. After you've selected the file you'd like to send, click the Send button.

2 First, you'll probably want to establish a chat conversation with your chat buddy to discuss the file trade. Then, when you're ready to make the exchange, click on the Send File toolbar button to initiate the file transfer.

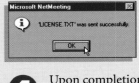

4 Upon completion of the file transfer, NetMeeting opens a dialog box indicating a successful transfer. Simply click on the OK button and you're all finished.

6 When the other person clicks the Send File button, you'll see the transfer screen shown here while the file is transferred to your machine. Notice a progress bar denotes how much of the file transfer remains. Also displayed are the file name, where it's being saved, who it's from, and how many bytes (out of how many total) have been received. Pay special attention to the warning, "Some files can contain viruses or otherwise be harmful to your computer. It is important to be certain that this file is from a trustworthy source." If you indeed trust the source, click once on the Open button as soon as the file transfer is complete.

5 Now let's see how to receive and use a file sent from another person. As you can see, I've asked my friend Cory to send the file right back to me.

How to Fine-Tune NetMeeting Options

In this exercise, you'll learn a bit about the finer points of configuring NetMeeting options. Most folks will want to keep the default parameters of NetMeeting options, but you should at least know where the commands are for changing them and what they do.

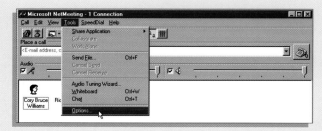

 1 From the main NetMeeting interface, click on Tools in the menu bar and scroll down to select Options.

▶ **Want to keep track of NetMeeting calls while working in other applications on your Desktop? You can configure NetMeeting to automatically notify you of incoming calls by clicking on the Properties tab marked General. Then select the first radio button under Incoming Calls.**

▶ **If your microphone sensitivity is too fine or too dull, click on the Audio tab in the Properties box. Then select the radio button marked "Let me adjust sensitivity myself." However, when you first configure NetMeeting, let it automatically adjust your microphone sensitivity; only adjust it yourself later on.**

▶ **Want to remain (relatively) anonymous? You can enter as much or as little information about yourself in the My Information section of NetMeeting Properties as you like. If you don't mind sharing information about yourself beyond name, e-mail address, and location, click in the Comments box and type in anything you'd like known about yourself.**

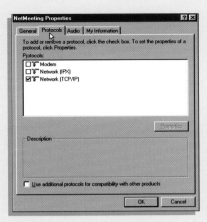

2 This opens the NetMeeting Properties box. There are four tabs which bring forth different options related to a particular topic. The first tab, General, includes options for displaying Net-Meeting on your desktop, notification of incoming calls, tweaking shared windows to fit your display, and a few file transfer options.

3 Click on the next tab button—Protocols. Here you'll see the different technologies that NetMeeting can use to connect your desktop to the online world. If you're working from home, there's a good chance you're using a modem and the first box will be checked. But if you're at work, or on a network, you're probably using either IPX or TCP/IP. You'll definitely want to leave these protocols as they are.

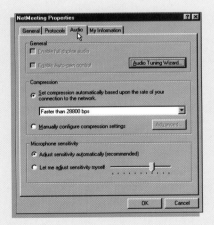

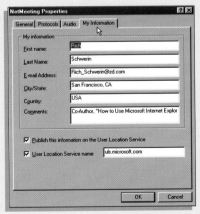

5 Click on the final tab, My Information. This is where you can edit the information about yourself that you first input at the beginning of this chapter. After making any changes or additions, click on the OK button to close NetMeeting Properties. Then stay online with NetMeeting for the final exercise in this chapter, "Using Internet Phone."

4 Click on the next tab, Audio, to see more information about the audio capabilities of NetMeeting. You'll learn more about these capabilities in the next exercise, "Using Internet Phone." You'll need a sound card, speakers, and microphone to take advantage of Internet Phone; for optimized audio compression, select the speed at which you're connecting. For now, accept the defaults as they are.

Using Internet Phone

So far you've traded text in the form of chat messages, and you've traded files back and forth. But another interesting—perhaps the most interesting—feature of Microsoft NetMeeting is its capability to send and receive audio data. You can have an audio conversation with NetMeeting much as you would over the phone, but the difference is that the cost of these calls is much lower than regular phone calls.

This exercise assumes you have a sound card, microphone, and speakers. As of this writing, not very many sound cards were supported by NetMeeting; here we'll walk you through setup and configuration. Then you'll place your first call on your own. Don't worry—it'll be easy and downright fun.

▶ **1** If you don't still have NetMeeting launched and running on your desktop, launch it now by double-clicking on the NetMeeting shortcut icon. Then, while in the main NetMeeting window, click on the Tools menu and scroll down to select Audio Tuning Wizard.

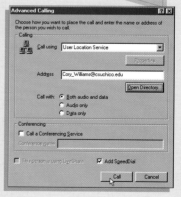

8 From the Advanced Calling box, you'll see you can place three types of calls: both audio and data, audio only, or data only. Select "Both audio and data" by clicking on the radio button. Then enter the address of the person you'd like to call. If you're not sure of that person's address, click once on the Open Directory button to see the alphabetical list of users connected to the Microsoft User Location Server, where you can simply click on the user's name to begin your audio call, just as you did throughout this chapter.

7 Get back to the main NetMeeting window, open the Call menu, and select Place Advanced Call.

2 Like any other Windows Wizard, the Audio Tuning Wizard walks you through the steps of tuning your audio settings so that you can enjoy Internet Phone calls using Microsoft NetMeeting. After reading the initial Wizard screen, click on the Next button.

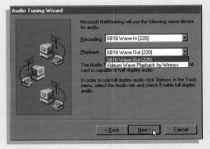

3 The Audio Wizard automatically detects your sound card or sound device. Should you have multiple devices to choose from, you can simply click on the pull-down menus and make your choice. You must make two different selections—one for recording and one for playback. You'll probably want to accept the defaults for both recording and for playback. Click on the Next button when you're ready to proceed.

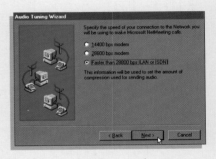

4 In the third step of the Audio Tuning Wizard, you're asked to select the speed at which you're connecting while using Microsoft NetMeeting. If you're at home, you're probably using either a 14.4Kbps modem or a 28.8Kbps modem. If you're at work, or on a network, select the third option, Faster than 28800bps (LAN or ISDN). Then click on the Next button.

6 You should now have successfully completed tuning your audio settings. The last screen of the Wizard provides some feedback about your microphone volume (based on the audio test you performed in the previous step). Click on the Finish button and you're ready to place your first Internet phone call.

5 Finally, the Audio Tuning Wizard steps you through the process of tuning your audio settings, both speaker and microphone volume. When you're ready to start a sample 9-second recording, click on the Start Recording button.

CHAPTER 16

Using the Whiteboard

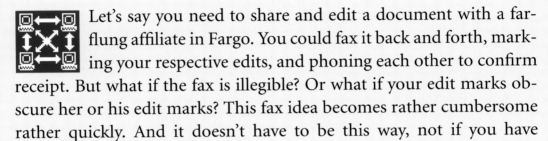 Let's say you need to share and edit a document with a far-flung affiliate in Fargo. You could fax it back and forth, marking your respective edits, and phoning each other to confirm receipt. But what if the fax is illegible? Or what if your edit marks obscure her or his edit marks? This fax idea becomes rather cumbersome rather quickly. And it doesn't have to be this way, not if you have Microsoft NetMeeting.

In the previous chapter, you learned about NetMeeting's text and audio communication capabilities. In this chapter, you'll explore another important function of NetMeeting: the shared Whiteboard. You can think of NetMeeting's Whiteboard as just a regular whiteboard in your office—a space to draw, share ideas and documents, and collaborate. But NetMeeting's Whiteboard is virtual. It exists as shared bits between your NetMeeting client and your friends NetMeeting client, and it doesn't matter where you and your friend are located—around the block or around the world.

How to Initiate a Whiteboard Session

In this first exercise, you'll initiate a Whiteboard session with a friend, and learn more about the basic whiteboarding tools available with NetMeeting. If you're not still online using NetMeeting from the previous chapter, launch NetMeeting now by double-clicking on the NetMeeting shortcut on your Desktop.

▶ **1** As you learned in the previous chapter, launching NetMeeting connects you (by default) to the Microsoft User Location Service. You'll need to find someone to share a Whiteboard with; in this example, Rich is in a call with his colleague Kyla. Then, click on the Whiteboard icon in the NetMeeting toolbar.

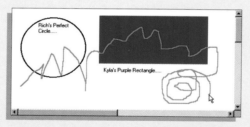

8 Use the Draw tool by clicking once in the shared Whiteboard. Then, drag with the mouse to draw or doodle on the Whiteboard. When you're finished, leave things where they are and go to the next lesson.

7 You can also draw and doodle on the shared Whiteboard space. Click on the Draw button. Notice that one is blue and one is yellow. You can select either one, and then your partner selects the remaining tool. The same is true of the remote pointer, which you'll learn about later in this chapter.

2 Now you'll see the shared Whiteboard screen (as will the person you're connected with). Anything you draw, type, or doodle will be accessible and visible to the other person. Notice the toolbar down the left side of the Whiteboard interface. Click on the Unfilled circle button and your cursor changes into a crosshair.

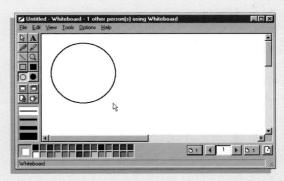

3 Click within the Whiteboard, and then drag to draw an unfilled circle. Release the mouse button and voila—your circle is complete.

4 Now click on the Text tool (marked with an *A*) at the top of the Whiteboard toolbar. Notice that your cursor now changes into an input-text cursor.

5 Click within the unfilled circle you just drew and type a message to your Whiteboard friend. Then press Enter.

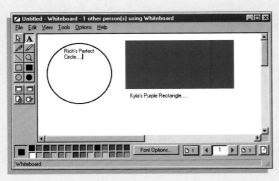

6 Your Whiteboard partner can also share information. Here Kyla selected the filled square tool and drew a rectangle. Then she clicked on the purple box in the colorbar, making the rectangle purple. Let your Whiteboard partner explore similar features.

How to Share Captured Screens

Doodling and drawing are fun Whiteboard features, but if you're not much of an artist, the thrill is quickly gone. As you just learned, you can also easily share text and draw shapes with different colors. But what if you want to share a screen shot or section of a screen from your Desktop or some other application?

NetMeeting's Whiteboard also lets you share screens quickly and easily. Here you'll clear the mess you just generated, and then you'll share an area from your Desktop and an entire window from an application on your Desktop.

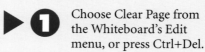

▶ **❶** Choose Clear Page from the Whiteboard's Edit menu, or press Ctrl+Del.

❾ Notice that whichever window you clicked on now appears in the shared Whiteboard space; your partner sees it, too.

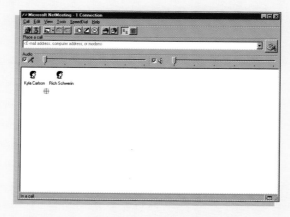

❽ The next window you click on will be transferred to your shared Whiteboard space. In this example, I've clicked in the NetMeeting window. Choose any window open on your desktop and click in it once.

2 Click on Yes to confirm that you want to clear the page.

3 Choose Select Area from the Tools menu and click on OK in the resulting dialog box. This changes your cursor into a crosshair.

4 Drag to select an area of your desktop. Here I've selected six shortcut icons from my Windows 95 desktop. When you're done selecting, release the mouse button.

5 Once you release the mouse button, the area you selected automatically appears in the shared Whiteboard window for your partner to see.

7 Click on OK. Your cursor turns into a complex crosshair icon.

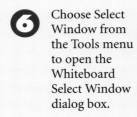

6 Choose Select Window from the Tools menu to open the Whiteboard Select Window dialog box.

How to Use the Remote Pointer and Lock Content

It's nice to share, but sometimes you'll need to show and tell instead. In this lesson, you'll learn to use the remote pointer tool and you'll also learn to lock content.

The remote pointer is a floating, colored hand icon that you can use to indicate the finer points of some shared information with your partner. The content locking feature lets you prevent your partner from editing any of the shared content in the Whiteboard area.

On these pages you'll create a simple map of cross streets, and then you'll use the remote pointer and content locking features to give directions to your partner.

TIP SHEET

▶ **It's useful to lock contents when you don't want the other person to change, edit, or alter information you're sharing in the Whiteboard space. But how can you tell if you've been locked out? Have your partner lock you out, and then try clicking on the Whiteboard space with any tool. You'll see a small lock icon, denoting that you're locked out.**

▶ **Clearing pages is as easy as pressing Ctrl+Del.**

▶ **You'll sometimes want to save Whiteboard documents for future use, but unfortunately you can only reopen and use these files (which have the extension .wht) using the NetMeeting Whiteboard. In contrast, you can open NetMeeting chat transcripts (.csv files) in any word processor or text editor such as WordPad or Notepad.**

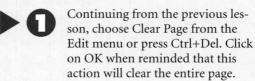

1 Continuing from the previous lesson, choose Clear Page from the Edit menu or press Ctrl+Del. Click on OK when reminded that this action will clear the entire page.

9 When the Save As dialog box appears, name the file whatever you like (map.wht, for instance) and save it in whichever directory you prefer. Then click on Save.

8 You can also easily save your Whiteboard work for future use. Choose Save As from the File menu.

7 A brief dialog box explains that the Whiteboard contents are being locked. If you change your mind, you can always click on Cancel.

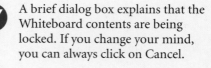

2 Starting with a clean Whiteboard space, click on the Line tool.

3 Drag in a horizontal direction to draw a horizontal line. When your line has reached the desired length, release the mouse button. Then click on the Text tool, click near the line you just created, and type the name of your street.

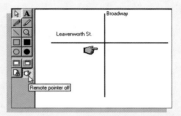

4 Now click on the Line tool again. Draw a perpendicular line in the Whiteboard space and then release the mouse button. Click on the Remote pointer tool and the colored remote pointer hand icon appears.

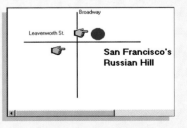

6 Although it's easy to point out information to your Whiteboard partner, sometimes you won't want to let your partner edit or change information in the Whiteboard screen. In this case, simply click on the Lock Contents button.

5 Your Whiteboard partner also has access to a remote pointer hand icon of a different color. Here my Whiteboard partner has entered some text (Broadway, San Francisco's Russian Hill) and drawn a filled-in circle where my apartment is. Notice the other remote pointer hand icon.

How to Share Applications

There seems to be no end to the useful collaboration tools incorporated into Microsoft's NetMeeting. In addition to chat, Whiteboard, and telephony capabilities, you can use NetMeeting to share applications with others. For example, if you have the latest copy of Doom or some other game and your NetMeeting partner doesn't, you can share and collaborate, giving that person full access to any application open on your Desktop.

Now you'll share an application, and open it for collaboration, with your NetMeeting partner. You'll practice by sharing Hearts, an accessory game that ships with every copy of Windows 95. But you could just as easily share a word processor, spreadsheet, e-mail application, or any other software from your system.

▶ ❶ From the main NetMeeting interface, while you're still connected with a partner, click on the Share Application toolbar button.

TIP SHEET

▶ **Sharing programs can bring to light difference in screen resolution between your system and your partners'. Even if your computer has a higher resolution, your scrolling area is limited by that of the computer with the lower resolution. If the window of a shared program scrolls off the window of a computer with a lower resolution, the hidden part of the window cannot be seen on your computer either.**

▶ **If you share a Windows Explorer window, such as My Computer or a folder on your computer, remember that you will be sharing all the Windows Explorer windows you have open.**

▶ **If you want your partner to see, but not control, your shared application, choose Work Alone from the Tools menu.**

 Look at the screen in the monitor in the center of the page. The Kyla Carlson box at the upper-right corner of the Microsoft Hearts Network box indicates that Kyla is using the application. When you've finished collaborating and sharing, simply close the window of the application. But maintain your partner connection for the next, and final, lesson.

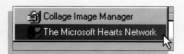

2 A drop-down list of all applications available for sharing appears. This list includes all open applications on your Desktop (in this example, Collage Image Manager and the Microsoft Hearts Network). Share Hearts by clicking on it.

3 A dialog box warns you that you're about to share an application. Click on OK.

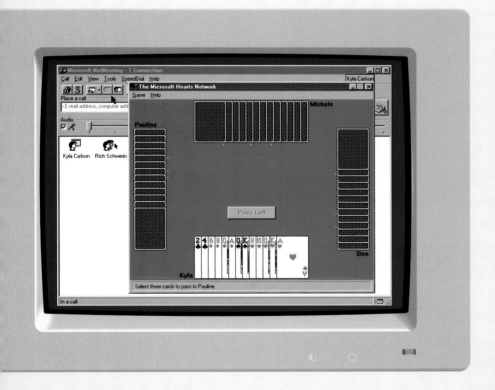

4 Sharing an application simply lets your partner see it. To let your partner use it, choose Collaborate from the Tools menu or click on the Collaborate toolbar button.

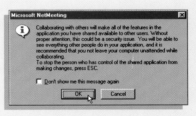

5 The next dialog box explains that not only are you sharing an application, you're collaborating with others. This is indeed a security risk, allowing someone else to take control of an application on your system. But it's just Hearts; what could possibly go wrong? Click on OK.

6 Because you've selected Share Application and Collaborate, the user icons in the NetMeeting window have changed. In this example, Rich Schwerin's icon now has a second, shadow icon, representing collaboration, and Kyla Carlson's icon has an application rectangle, meaning she's using an application that I've shared with her.

How to Talk, Chat, and Use the Whiteboard Simultaneously

Just like Windows 95, most people can multitask with ease. Whether you're driving down the road listening to the radio or watching TV while ironing, it's not too difficult to do several things at once. Microsoft NetMeeting makes multitasking particularly easy.

In this final lesson, you'll see how simple it is to carry on a chat conversation while whiteboarding. You'll need your good old NetMeeting partner, and together, you'll chat and whiteboard simultaneously, pulling together the skills you've mastered in the previous lessons and in the previous chapter.

▶ **1** From the main NetMeeting window, click on the Chat toolbar button.

▸ **If your NetMeeting window gets crowded with both the Chat and Whiteboard windows open, simply resize those windows into side-by-side rectangles by dragging on their borders.**

▸ **Having trouble reading the text in your Chat or Whiteboard window? From within the Chat window, choose Font from the Options menu, and do the same thing (choose Options, Font) from within the Whiteboard window. The Font dialog box lets you change fonts, point sizes, and colors quickly and easily.**

2 You'll see the familiar chat window you saw in the previous chapter. Enter a few friendly missives ("Hi, Kyla," "Hola, Ricardo") and press Enter.

3 To add the shared Whiteboard to your chat conversation, simply click on the Whiteboard toolbar button.

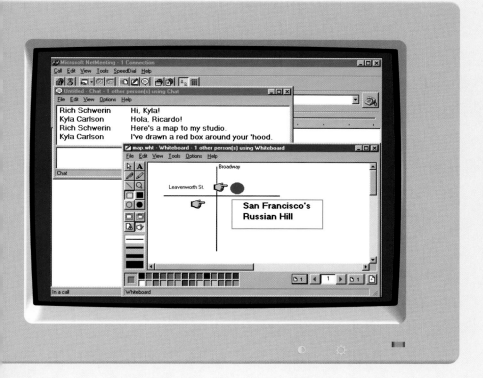

4 You'll see the Whiteboard content from your previous lesson (map.wht), along with remote pointers. Unlock the content by clicking on the Lock Content button.

5 As you chat in the chat window, you can also continue to work in the shared Whiteboard window, making relevant comments (for example, Kyla's edit of my San Francisco map). When you're finished multitasking, quit NetMeeting entirely by closing both windows and then shut down NetMeeting by pulling down the Call menu and choosing Exit.

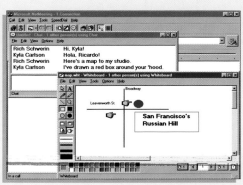

CHAPTER 17

Getting to Know HTML

 By now you've probably discovered that surfing graphical Web pages with Internet Explorer is fun and easy. But did you ever stop to think about the underlying technologies that work together to make it all possible? In this chapter, you'll step back for a moment and learn a little about one of the fundamental components of Web pages—Hypertext Markup Language (HTML), the *lingua franca* of the World Wide Web.

HTML is the language used to create documents for the World Wide Web. Although most browsers will display any document that is written in plain text, there are advantages to using HTML. Documents written with HTML can include formatting, graphics, links to other documents, and much more.

HTML is really quite simple, but at first glance the HTML code (also known as *tags*) can seem confusing and mysterious. In this chapter, you'll learn the basics as we demystify HTML together. For starters, you'll take a look at the actual source code of the PC Computing Web site, and exploring the functions of some of these HTML source tags. You'll also explore several Web sites that will help you learn more about HTML, and then download a few HTML creation programs.

How to View and Understand HTML

First, we'll take a behind-the-scenes look at a Web page to show you how HTML works. Though at first it may seem complicated, HTML is actually much simpler than any programming language. HTML tags tell the browser that views the Web page how the graphics, text, and other elements are to behave. These tags open with a less-than symbol (<) and close with a greater-than symbol (>).

Now let's take a look at the HTML source code for of *PC Computing* magazine's main home page, which offers a wide variety of tags and examples and will serve as a handy tutorial. However, you can just as easily use the lesson you learn here to investigate the source code of any Web page.

TIP SHEET

▶ **Who makes up all these HTML tags, anyway? HTML was developed by a group of physicists in Switzerland who were looking to collaborate and communicate quickly and easily. HTML has since expanded to include a wide variety of tags that perform an array of functions.**

▶ **You will find that some HTML tags are not supported by all browsers. In the interest of keeping ahead of the competition, browsers are constantly being updated to include new tags beyond those included in the HTML standard. For example, the <BLINK> tag, which causes text to blink on the page, is not supported by many browsers.**

▶ **All tags (with the exception of the <P>, or paragraph, tag) come in pairs of starting and ending tags. For example, the <BODY> tag (denoting body text) consists of the <BODY> tag at the beginning of the text and the </BODY> tag at the end.**

▶ **HTML isn't case-sensitive; that is, the command remains the same regardless of whether you type <BODY> or <body>.**

 You should have Internet Explorer up and running. Click once in the Address box, enter the URL **www.pccomputing.com**, and press Enter.

10 In the last section of the source, you'll see a mailto command. This command sets up an instant hypertext link that launches a person's mail client so that shecan send e-mail to a particular address almost instantaneously. Also notice the close command (</html>), which marks the end of an HTML page. When you're finished scanning the source, click on the Close (X) button in the upper right-hand corner of the Editor box.

 Notice in this section the different alignment commands (for example, ALIGN=CENTER) and width commands (for example, BORDER=0 HEIGHT=31 WIDTH=88), as well as commands for changing font colors, which are represented by numbers.

2 Click once on the View menu, then scroll down and select Source.

3 A simple text editor appears with an open file of HTML code. Click on the Edit menu, then scroll select Word Wrap. This will allow you to see more of the text at one time.

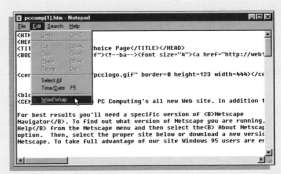

4 The first thing you'll notice at the top of the source code is the <HTML> tag. This tells the browser that the document is written with HTML. The next tag, <HEAD>, lets the browser know that the following tag will be the title of the page, which is specified by the <TITLE> tag. This sets the title headline, íPC Computing Choice Page.î The rest of the text in the paragraph specifies an advertising banner, which is a clickable image often used for advertising purposes.

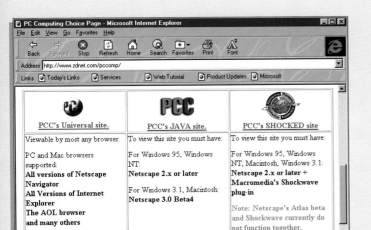

5 The next tag, <CENTER>, is used used to center elements—text, graphics, and so on—on a Web page.

6 The <BLOCKQUOTE> tag sets off a block of text from the rest of the page; in this example, it places the bold, centered text introduction to the PC Computing site just after the PCC logo.

8 The middle "frame," or table cell, uses a simple command to give the appearance of what the PC Computing Shockwave site looks like (notice the command <img src="shkloop.giv">, which denotes the GIF animation loop).

7 The next three sections contain the instructions for a special kind of table that looks like a frame. You've seen a lot of framed Web sites thus far; frames are an effective way of managing and designing Web sites to make them easier to navigate and comprehend. However, not all browsers support frames, and this Web site must be universally accessible, so tables were used instead so browsers of all types could view the page.

How to Teach Yourself HTML

With a basic knowledge of HTML in hand, let's surf to several sites that will help you learn more about HTML. If you find these brief introductions of interest, you can pursue your HTML education further. However, it's not necessary to dig deeply into HTML to use Internet Explorer to its fullest capabilities.

 ❶ Type the following URL into Internet Explorer's Address box, then press Enter: **web.canlink.com/webdesign**.

❾ Now you're reading Eamonn Sullivan's Crash Course on Writing Documents for the Web. Click on your Favorites menu icon button and scroll down to select Add to Favorites. Accept the default name by clicking on OK.

❽ Now scroll further down through the list of HTML-related links and click on the link *Crash Course on Web Documents*.

TIP SHEET

▶ The sites you surf to in this lesson just scratch the surface of a multitude of sites on the Web designed to help you learn HTML. If you're really interested, check out *How to Use HTML3* by Scott Arpajian (Ziff-Davis Press, 1996).

▶ While Internet Explorer's text editor is useful for the most simple tasks, serious HTML coders might consider working with a more powerful editor designed to make more advanced coding easier. In the next few lessons you'll be downloading some of these tools, including Microsoft Internet Assistant for Word and DeltaPoint QuickSite.

2 Add the Web Designer page to your list of Favorites by clicking on the Favorites button, scrolling down, and selecting Add to Favorites.

3 Accept the default name by clicking on the OK button in the resulting dialog box.

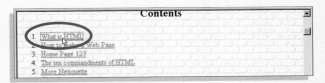

4 Scroll down through the Web Designer site until you see the Contents section. Click on the first link you see, *What is HTML?*

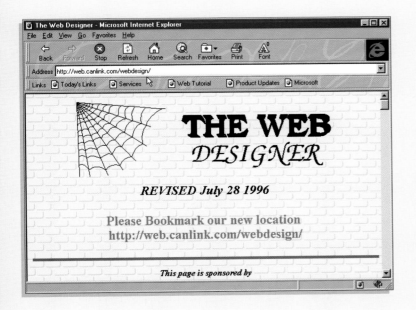

5 A list of links appears. Click on the link Learning HTML. This takes you to a very useful HTML tutorial site, which you might want to explore later at your own pace.

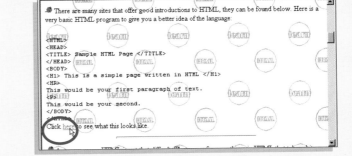

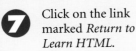

7 Click on the link marked *Return to Learn HTML.*

6 Scroll down until you see a section with HTML source code written directly on the Web page. At the bottom of this code, click on the word *here* in the line "Click here to see what this looks like." This will show you the result of the source code.

How to Download and Install Internet Assistant for Word (Part I)

You know how to use a word processor. In fact, you probably know how to use Microsoft Word. If so, you can create basic Web pages quickly and easily using Microsoft's Internet Assistant for Word.

In this lesson, which you'll want to skip if you don't have a copy of Microsoft Word, you'll download Internet Assistant for Word, and install and configure it. Internet Assistant is absolutely free, and can be used to create simple Web pages. It can also enable Microsoft Word to browse Web pages.

Since this download is a bit complicated, we've broken it up in to two parts. In this first part, you'll find and download the software; in the next part, you'll install, configure and launch it.

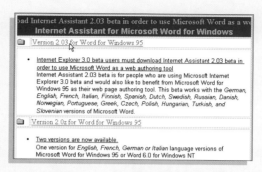

▶ ❶ Enter the following URL into Internet Explorer's Address box: **www.microsoft .com/msword/internet/ia**. This takes you to the Microsoft Internet Assistant for Word download page. Click on the Version 2.0.3 link (or the most current version available).

TIP SHEET

▸ **Internet technology changes quickly, so don't be surprised if the version of Internet Assistant—which as of this writing is 2.0.3—has been upgraded.**

▸ **If you don't have Microsoft Word, don't worry. Corel's WordPerfect also offers a free add-on, which you can find at www.wordperfect.com.**

▸ **The Windows 95 version isn't the only version of Internet Assistant available for free at the Microsoft site. Your Macintosh-enabled friends can grab a free copy of Microsoft Internet Assistant for Word for Macintosh, as well.**

❷ After reading the setup instructions, click on the link marked Download. Click on OK in the resulting dialog box.

❸ The Save As dialog box opens. Be sure to save the Internet Assistant for Word executable in your Windows Temp file. Then click on the Save button.

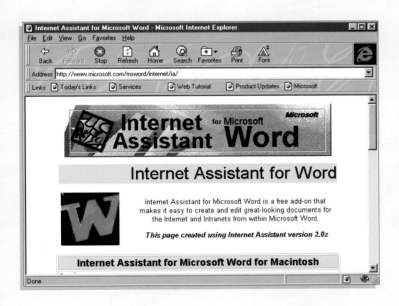

❹ Watch as Internet Assistant for Word is downloaded to your hard drive.

❺ When it's finished downloading, click once on the Windows 95 Taskbar's Start button, then scroll up and select Run.

❻ In the Run dialog box's Open window, type in the following path: **C:\TEMP\wdia203z.exe**. (If the version has changed, substitute the file name the most current version.) Then click on OK. *(Continued on page 194.)*

How to Download and Install Internet Assistant for Word (Part II)

Now let's install and configure Microsoft Internet Assistant for Word. And, provided you have Microsoft Word available on your Desktop, you'll launch Internet Assistant as well, and check out what it's like to view Web pages from within your word processor.

▶ ❶ Click on the Continue button.

❽ Now you'll see a Web page right from within the Microsoft Word interface. You can continue to explore Internet Assistant for Word's features on your own.

TIP SHEET

▶ **Once you've successfully installed and configured Microsoft Internet Assistant for Word, you'll notice several changes and additions to the Word interface. Among these, notice the File menu's extra selections—Open URL and Browse Web.**

▶ **Also notice the small glasses icon button to the far left of Word's toolbar. If you click on this, you switch from word processing to Web page creation mode, and the button changes to a pencil. Click again on the pencil icon button to switch back to word processing mode.**

▶ **With Internet Assistant for Word, it's easy to create basic Web pages from scratch. But since you're already in a word processing interface, you can also quickly and easily convert existing Word documents to Web documents with the click of a button.**

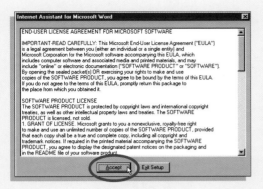

2 Read the licensing agreement carefully, then click on the Accept button.

3 Click on the Install button to continue.

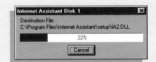

4 Watch closely as Microsoft Internet Assistant for Word is installed to your hard drive.

5 Click on the Launch Word button to start up your copy of Word.

6 Once Word has been launched, click on OK.

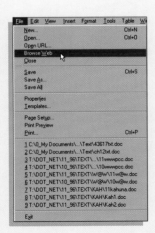

7 From within the Microsoft Word interface, click on the File menu, then scroll down and select Browse the Web.

How to Download and Install DeltaPoint QuickSite

Microsoft Internet Assistant for Word is very useful, and it's free! But for more complicated Web sites, and for an easier user interface, you'll want to try some different tools. One such tool is DeltaPoint's award-winning QuickSite.

DeltaPoint offers a free 30-day trial version for free download. On this page, you'll download and configure your own copy of QuickSite. You'll then continue the installation and configuration process, as well as create a nice Web page of your own, in the next Try It! section.

TIP SHEET

▶ **DeltaPoint QuickSite does *not* require that you know any HTML code. It's an instant Web page construction tool kit that lets you build, test, and install your Web page with a few clicks of the mouse.**

▶ **Remember, this copy of QuickSite that you downloaded in this lesson is not free. It's a 30-day trial version—if you decide to keep it, the cost is $99. If you don't, your trial version will *time out*—that is, stop working—after 30 days.**

▶**❶** Enter the following URL in Internet Explorer's Address box: www.deltapoint.com/qsdown/qs01000.htm. Then press Enter.

❽ Click on OK in the resulting dialog box. This immediately begins the installation of DeltaPoint QuickSite, which we don't want to do quite yet, so click on the Exit Install button. You'll finish installing QuickSite and use it to create your first Web site in the next Try It! section.

❼ Since QuickSite is a zipped executable file, you have the option of unzipping it in the Temp folder. Click on the Unzip button to do so.

2 Scroll down through this page until you see several links to download QuickSite, marked qssetup.exe. Click one of these links.

3 As Internet Explorer begins to download DeltaPoint's QuickSite, click on OK to save it to disk.

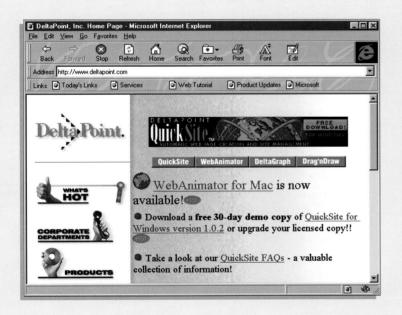

4 You can choose to save QuickSite in the same Temp directory as you saved Microsoft's Internet Assistant for Word in the last lesson. Click once on the Save button. (It does take a while for Internet Explorer to download QuickSite, because it's a rather large file. But it's worth the wait.)

5 When QuickSite is finished downloading, run it by selecting the Windows 95 Taskbar Start button, scrolling up, and selecting Run.

6 In the Run dialog box, type **c:\Temp\qssetup.exe** in the Open window, then press Enter.

TRY IT!

Now that you've downloaded DeltaPoint QuickSite (Chapter 17), you'll install and configure it, and use it to create a Web page of your own.

To finish the installation and configuration job on DeltaPoint's QuickSite that you began in the last lesson of Chapter 17, choose Run from the Start menu, type **c:\qsettup\setup.exe** in the Open box, and press Enter.

2

To begin the DeltaPoint QuickSite installation,

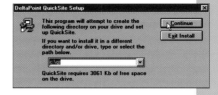

click on Continue. A progress indicator will show that QuickSite is installing itself.

To create a separate QuickSite group, click on the Create button. Click on OK once you're told that the installation is complete.

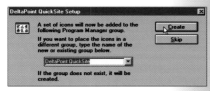

From the DeltaPoint QuickSite program group, double-click on the DeltaPoint QuickSite icon to launch QuickSite.

Read the licensing agreement carefully and click on the Agree button.

Since you don't yet have a serial number, you can simply try QuickSite for 30 days. Click on the Cancel button to display the QuickSite interface.

Register DeltaPoint QuickSite

Please enter your registration number:

- / -

The registration number is on your program disk or was provided when you purchased QuickSite.

If you do not enter a registration number you have 30 days remaining to evaluate QuickSite.

Take a few moments to visit the QuickSite home page at http://www.deltapoint.com

Call us at 800-446-6955 or 408-648-4000.

E-Mail us - Sales_Support@deltapoint.com

Enter   Cancel   Help

Choose New Project from the File menu.

Type **HomePage** in the Project Name box and then click on the Create button. Click on Yes in the resulting dialog box to use QuickSite's handy site creation Wizard.

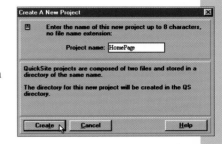

Type **My First Home Page** in the text window and then click on Next.

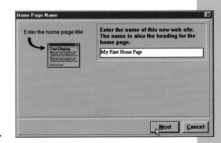

In the next dialog box, click in the text window and type **Hello! And Welcome to My First Web Site, created using DeltaPoint's QuickSite software and How to Use Microsoft Internet Explorer by S.G. Hubert and Rich Schwerin.** Then click on Next.

Continue to next page ▶

TRY IT!

Continue below

 Click on the Next button in the Lines And Dates dialog box. In the Automatic E-Mail Icon dialog box, type your e-mail address (optional) in the text box. Then click on Next.

 Accept the default Web site structure by clicking on Next. Click on Next again in the initial Page Style dialog box.

 Click on the Background button to change your background graphic.

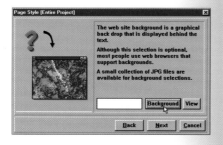

 Click on the qs_rock.gif GIF file in the qs\gifs directory, click on OK, and then click on Next in the resulting dialog box.

 Choose Green from the Header Line drop-down list box to select a different line color.

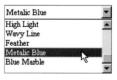

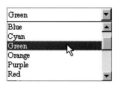 Choose Metalic Blue from the Footer Line drop-down list and then click on Next.

Select a different bullet design by choosing Black Ball from the Bullet List Item drop-down list. Click on Next.

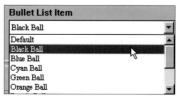

18

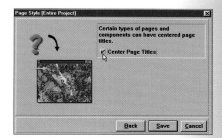

Click on the Center Page Titles check box to select it. Then click on Save.

19

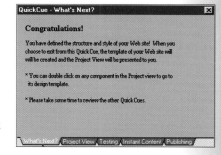

You'll see a QuickCue window with several tabs. Read the information on the What's Next? tab. Then click on the various other tabs to review their contents, too. When you're done, close the QuickCue by clicking on its Close box.

20

Now you're almost ready to view the page you just created. Click on the lightning bolt icon or press Ctrl+B.

21

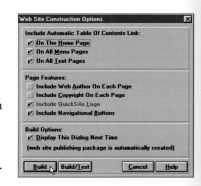

Accept the defaults in the Web Site Construction Options dialog box and click on the Build button.

22

Choose Test Web Site from the Project menu.

23

Click on Yes to set Internet Explorer as your default browser.

24

Find the file marked iexplore.exe, select it, and click on OK. (In case you're wondering, iexplore.exe should be installed in C:\Program Files\Microsoft Internet by default.)

25

Voila! Here is what you accomplished in just a few easy steps. As you can see, QuickSite truly is Quick. Now you can use it to built even more complicated sites on your own.

APPENDIX

Internet Access Providers

 In addition to the Microsoft Network, to which you have access directly from your Desktop (along with 30 free hours for new subscribers), here are a few Internet access providers (ISPs) in the U.S. and Canada. Look for a provider that gives you a flat monthly rate (usually around $20), or you'll end up with very unpleasant surprises when you get your monthly bill. And, of course, ask the sales representative whether the provider supports or provides a special version of Internet Explorer.

AlterNet

http://ww.uu.net/
(800) 488-6384 U.S.
(800) 463-8123 Canada

Concentric Network Corporation

http://www.concentric.net/
(800) 939-4262 U.S.

EarthLink Network

http://www.earthlink.net/
(800) 395-8425 U.S.

IBM Global Network

http://www.ibm.com/
globalnetwork/
(800) 775-5808 U.S. and
Canada

PSINet, Inc.

http://www.psi.net/
(800) 827-7482 U.S.

The Well, Inc.

http://www.well.com/
(415) 332-9200 U.S. and Canada

TheOnRamp Group, Inc.

http://www.theonramp.net/
(800) 603-2721 U.S. and Canada

WorldNet

http://www.worldnet.com/
(800) 967-5363 U.S.

INDEX